Bre

Strategies for Overcoming
Spiritual Bondage

Compiled and Edited by Katy Kauffman

Lighthouse Bible Studies

Scripture references marked ESV are taken from The Holy Bible, English Standard Version. ESV® Permanent Text Edition® (2016). Copyright © 2001 by Crossway Bibles, a publishing ministry of Good News Publishers.

Scripture references marked KJV are taken from the Holy Bible, King James Version.

Scripture references marked NASB are taken from the New American Standard Bible. Copyright © 1960, 1962, 1963, 1968, 1971, 1972, 1973, 1975, 1977, 1995 by The Lockman Foundation.

Scripture references marked NCV are taken from The Holy Bible, New Century Version®. Copyright © 2005 by Thomas Nelson, Inc.

Scripture references marked NIV are taken from the Holy Bible, New International Version®, NIV® Copyright ©1973, 1978, 1984, 2011 by Biblica, Inc.® Used by permission. All rights reserved worldwide.

Scripture references marked NKJV are taken from the New Kings James Version. Copyright © 1979, 1980,1982 by Thomas Nelson, Inc. Used by permission. All rights reserved.

Scripture references marked NLT are taken from the Holy Bible, New Living Translation copyright© 1996, 2004, 2007 by Tyndale House Publishers Inc.

Cover designed by Katy Kauffman, Lighthouse Bible Studies, LLC

Cover Photo Copyright © RomoloTavani. Used under license from istock.com.

Interior photos on all pages are public domain photos from pixabay.com, except the photos on pages 33 and 124 provided by Josie Siler.

Published by Lighthouse Bible Studies, LLC,
P.O. Box 304, Buford, Georgia 30515

ISBN: 0-9896112-7-2

ISBN-13: 978-0-9896112-7-5

Dedication

This book is dedicated to every soul who longs for freedom.
God is great enough to set you free.

Contents

Strategies for Overcoming Twenty-Five Forms of Spiritual Bondage

Short Stories

Breaking Free and Staying Free

Acknowledgements

I would like to thank every author who contributed to this project. To those who participated in the original blog series, it's a blessing to see God turn our series into a book. To those who joined us for the book project, thank you for saying yes to the adventure.

I would also like to thank every pastor, Bible teacher, godly parent, and faithful friend who has helped us to break chains and overcome hang ups. Your words are priceless.

Most of all, I would like to thank the Lord Jesus Christ, our heavenly Father, and the Holy Spirit—our God, three in one. You are greater than any obstacle, fiercer than any monster, and stronger than any storm. Thank You for rescuing us from dangers and despair. May the truths You've shown us and made a reality in our lives, bring freedom and healing to many.

~Katy Kauffman

Introduction
A Dream to Be Free

Introduction: A Dream to Be Free

We dream of many things in life—perhaps of marriage, children, adventure, or success—but have you ever dreamt of freedom?

> "When the LORD brought back the captivity of Zion, we were like those who dream."
> Psalm 126:1 NKJV

Just like God's people in the Old Testament longed for freedom from captivity and oppression, God's children today long to be free of spiritual bondage. Our spiritual enemies, numerous and powerful, war against our souls, and only in Christ can we resist them. Some enemies slither their way into our lives, stealthy and silent. Others, with earthshaking roars, pounce on us. Bondage can start in many ways, but freedom doesn't have to be an ideal we just dream about. It can be a reality.

It is our prayer that if you are dreaming of freedom, this book gives you strategies to break your chains. Only God has the power to free us from spiritual bondage. Each of us who has contributed to this book knows that. Yet God wants us to be actively involved in the dream of freedom. Our poor choices allow chains to grow, but our wise choices and God's power dissolve them. So take heart, fellow believer. Freedom is on the horizon.

You may want to read this book on your own, either in your quiet time or when you have spare moments on the go. But if you are feeling the chains of spiritual bondage grow tighter and tighter around your heart, I suggest that you find a friend to read with you. Satan, one of our greatest spiritual enemies, seeks to isolate us from the help and hope we desperately need. Don't let him succeed. If you are struggling with a bad habit, sin, or crippling way of thinking or feeling, tell a godly person you trust. Ask him or her to read a devotion or two of this book with you, and then talk together about what you've read. We are stronger when we fight together than when we strive apart.

If you or someone you love is struggling with the will to live, we want you to get help as soon as possible. Call this number to receive instant help: 1-800-273-TALK (8255). (This is the National Suicide Prevention Lifeline. Also visit the website for help: suicidepreventionlifeline.org.) Your life is too precious to handle this on your own. God treasures you, and He will help you to win this fight if you look to Him. These Scripture verses prove it: Psalm 9:10, 18:17, 18:28-39, 27:14, 32:7, 37:23-24, 42:5, 50:15, 55:18, 56:9, 61:2, 62:8, 71:3, 73:26, 94:17-19, 107:14, 116:8, 138:3, 138:8, 147:3; Isaiah 40:28-31, 41:10; 2 Timothy 1:7, 4:17-18; Hebrews 4:16, 13:5-6; James 4:7-8; 1 John 5:4.

If you are in need of encouragement to win your spiritual battles, keep reading. You will find articles on how to break specific forms of spiritual bondage. There is also a section giving more principles for how to break chains, such as the principle of displacement. Another section is filled with short stories that illustrate the need to be free and how the character in the story realized the dream.

Victory is possible because God makes it possible. It takes His work and our cooperation. We have to want it, more than our own way, more than what we can make of life on our own. It takes courage, time, truth, and the power of God. May you find in this book hope that becomes reality and freedom that brings relief and joy to the weary soul.

Sow the help of God into your daily battles, and reap a harvest of victory.

"When the LORD brought back the captivity of Zion,
we were like those who dream.
Then our mouth was filled with laughter,
and our tongue with singing.
Then they said among the nations,
'The LORD has done great things for them.'
The LORD has done great things for us,
and we are glad.
Bring back our captivity, O LORD,
as the streams in the South.
Those who sow in tears shall reap in joy.
He who continually goes forth weeping,
bearing seed for sowing,
shall doubtless come again with rejoicing,
bringing his sheaves with him."
Psalms 126:1-6 NKJV

Strategies for Overcoming Twenty-Five Forms of Spiritual Bondage

Loosening the Grip of Fear
by Katy Kauffman

It stood tall and red in my dream. I backed away from the red monster and tried to get away, but the white room offered no way of escape—no doors, no windows. As my fear of the monster grew, he grew taller and scarier.

Then it hit me. "This is my dream. I don't have to be scared of you!"

The moment I said that, he started shrinking till he was just a red puddle on the floor. I stood above him, amazed that I had been afraid of something so puny. My fear of him gave him power over me, but in reality—or in my dream—he was nothing more than a red blob.

The more power we give to fear, the taller and scarier it grows in our lives. The more we say yes to fear, the tighter its grip on us becomes. But God didn't intend for fear to be our reality—not the kind of fear that paralyzes us and keeps us from living life to the fullest with Him.

Fear grows as we take our eyes off of the God who protects us and provides for us, and we focus on the worries and *what ifs* of life. *What if I don't have enough money to pay my bills? What if my marriage falls apart? What if I don't ever meet the right person? What if I try to make new friends but they reject me? What if I try to serve God and I fail? What if?*

In every *what if* of life, we need to count on God. We need to remember how much He loves us and wants to take care of us. Since God is watching over us, we can say no to fear and watch it become a puddle on the floor. We can loosen fear's grip on our souls by exercising the power, love, and sound mind that God gives us.

> "For God has not given us a spirit of fear,
> but of power and of love and of a sound mind."
> 2 Timothy 1:7 NKJV

God's power enables us to overcome the fear of failure.

God's love enables us to overcome the fear of rejection.

God's truth enables us to overcome the fear that comes with ignorance and wrong thinking.

In whatever way the great enemy of our souls, Satan, wants to enslave us with fear, God has an answer and a way of escape. By His power, we can overcome weakness and thoughts that we can't do what God wants us to do. By His love, we can overcome the fear of not being liked or accepted and we can go where He sends us and share His truth and love with others. By having a sound mind, we can refuse Satan's lies and trust that we are good enough in Christ to do God's will and God is good enough to keep His promise and provide for His children.

The Strategies

So when fear threatens to enslave you with no foreseeable way of escape, refuse its grip with these strategies:

1. Decide whether the fear is reasonable.

If so, pray for God's direction and help in dealing with the situation and ask for His protection. Move forward staying close to Him so you can easily hear Him and follow His lead. If it's an unreasonable fear, ask for God's help to put it out of your mind.

2. **Silence fear with the truth.**

Research what God's Word says about your particular fear, and depend on His promises and His power. Memorizing the verses may help shrink fear.

3. **Confide in a trusted, godly friend or spouse.**

Tell them about your fear, and ask them to help you see it from God's perspective. Be open to their objectivity, and see this fear as God does—a puny blob on the floor.

4. **Trust God that if He allows something difficult to happen in your life, He will work it for good (Romans 8:28).**

God's heart is too loving and His character is too good to allow it to happen otherwise. He only allows those things that make us braver, stronger, and more useful to His kingdom. This helped me to overcome being afraid of tragedies when I was a teenager. The good that God worked in my friends' lives, and in mine, helped me to overcome my fear of bad things happening. Looking back now, I can see how the *bad things* made my family closer, served as an important wake-up call, or deepened our faith and strengthened our endurance.

5. **Imagine your fear sitting next to God, and ask yourself who would win in a fight.**

Imagine fear sitting next to God's limitless power, His unsurpassed knowledge, His perfect love, and His vast omnipresence. Who do you think would win? Remember that God is so much bigger than any fear.

6. **Refuse the burden that fear places on your emotions by choosing the joy of faith.**

Trust God, stay close to His heart and under His "wing," and rest in the peace and joy that come with remembering He is your Daddy and your God.

Loosen fear's grip on your heart by remembering God's truth and love. Remember He fights for you and wants you to operate in the spirit He has given you. It's not a spirit of fear. Overcome fear with the power, love, and sound mind that God graciously supplies to us. Don't let fear win.

Silencing Guilt
by Katy Kauffman

She walked into the house, desperate to find Jesus. Her life had been filled with sin, guilt, and shame. The haunting melody of guilt had followed her, had crept into her soul. But she heard Jesus sing a different song, one of mercy and forgiveness. His words taught that it was possible to turn from sin and receive God's forgiveness. His actions showed that He cared for everyone, even a sinner like her. She understood the gospel and craved its mercy. She accepted its truth and turned from her lifestyle of sin and heartache. So she had to find Him.

This woman wanted to thank Jesus and show just how much she loved Him and the restoration He gave. When she found Jesus in the house, she knelt at His feet and wept. Her anguished soul found hope in the Savior. She dried His feet with her hair and anointed them with oil, costly oil. This was her gift of love to Him, but not everyone understood it.

In this house full of religious people, guilt's eerie melody started again, and the host of the home sang it.

> "Now when the Pharisee who had invited Him
> saw this, he spoke to himself, saying, 'This Man,
> if He were a prophet, would know who
> and what manner of woman this is who
> is touching Him, for she is a sinner'"
> (Luke 7:39 NKJV*).

Jesus answered the man with a story of two debtors. Both owed a creditor money, one a small sum and the other ten times that. Both debts were forgiven. Jesus asked the host who would love the creditor more. The Pharisee's answer was the debtor who had been forgiven more.

Then Jesus directed His song of mercy and forgiveness to the woman:

"Your sins are forgiven" (Luke 7:48),

and

"Your faith has saved you. Go in peace" (Luke 7:50).

Does the haunting melody of guilt follow you wherever you go? Does it steal your joy and keep you from drawing close to God? Have you heard any of guilt's lyrics before?

- *You can't draw close to God—you are too sinful.*
- *How many times have you given in to the same sin?*
- *You're not good enough for God to love you.*

Jesus' forgiveness silenced the melody of guilt for this woman in the Bible, and He can silence it for us. What lyrics are in Jesus' song?

- "As the Father loved Me, I also have loved you; abide in My love" (John 15:9).
- "Neither do I condemn you; go and sin no more" (John 8:11).
- "I have come as a light into the world, that whoever believes in Me should not abide in darkness" (John 12:46).
- "There is therefore now no condemnation for those who are in Christ Jesus, who do not walk according to the flesh, but according to the Spirit" (Romans 8:1).

Let God's song of love and forgiveness be the melody that you hear and hold onto. Drown out guilt's negative lyrics with His truth, and find rest and peace in His forgiveness. Be energized to follow Him daily, and never forget the reality that in Christ, you're forgiven and you're loved.

Implement these strategies to silence guilt in your life and to move forward with God in freedom and joy.

The Strategies

1. **Drown out guilt's haunting melody with God's song of love and forgiveness.** Read Scripture to remember your reality in Christ—you are forgiven (Ephesians 1:7), loved (1 John 4:19), accepted (Eph 1:6), and commissioned (Mark 16:15, Matthew 28:18-20).

2. **Move past the consciousness of your sin to drawing close to God** (Hebrews 10:19-22). God *wants* us to draw close to Him, and Jesus' death for our sins makes it possible.

3. **When you feel guilty because your past sins have affected someone else, trust God that He will take care of that person, and make amends if possible.** We can't undo our past actions, but we can choose good now, and we can ask God to help those affected by our poor choices.

4. **Don't let the past define you.** See yourself as God does (see Ephesians Chapter 1), and find your identity in Christ.

5. **Don't let the past keep you from serving God now.** Jesus graciously forgave and restored Peter after he had denied Jesus three times (John 21:15-17). Walk with God from this point forward, because He has work for you to do.

6. **Let go of the emotional turmoil that guilt causes, and walk in joy and gratefulness.** Feeling guilty or sorrowful over our sin is good so that we confess it and repent. But allowing guilt to imprison us and paralyze us is not. In the book of Nehemiah, when God's people understood in how many ways they had broken God's law, they wept. But God's message to them was to practice the ways of His Word and to have joy. His joy would be their strength (Nehemiah 8:10). Joy and

gratefulness give us strength to move past our forgiven sins to follow God and serve Him.

7. **Rest in the matchless love that God has for you.** He gave His Son so that you wouldn't have to suffer forever without Him. Find rest and peace in the love of God, and share His love with others. We can love much because we have been forgiven much.

*All Scripture verses are NKJV.

Escape the Prison of Anxiety
by Ginger Harrington

Am I going crazy?

For the first time in my life, sanity and peace seemed like a question instead of a given.

Years ago, I battled a hyperthyroid disorder. Plunging into the chaos of a thyroid-induced storm, adrenaline flooded my system, and I lived on the edge of panic.

It was an agony of slow months before my hands stopped shaking. And longer before I slept more than an hour or two at night.

Anxiety marched in with a take-all vengeance, and worry held me captive in my own home—

- Afraid to go out.
- Afraid to stay in.
- Afraid of being afraid.
- Afraid of nothing specific.
- Afraid of everything.

Anxiety wears many faces: apprehension, nervousness, worry, fear, and panic. It robs us of peace, making it hard to concentrate on simple tasks, make decisions, and stand firm in faith. Regardless of the cause, worry will become a prison if we do not learn powerful strategies to break the chains of toxic thinking.

You Are Not Alone in the Struggle

When worry batters our soul, God is our source of strength. We discover the reality of God's might in the midst of the hard things. Power to stand against fear is grounded in a present focus on God. Be still and know that He is God.

He is with us in the storm. "When you pass through the waters, I will be with you; and through the rivers, they will not overflow you" (Isaiah 43:2 NASB*). He will not forsake us, even when we lack faith or strength to overcome worry.

We may not be able to control our emotions, but we can choose how we will respond to worry. Rarely is there instant relief from the discomfort of anxiety, but feelings will eventually follow faith.

If there is a medical cause to your anxiety, be sure to talk to your doctor. Christian counseling for serious and persistent anxiety can be very helpful. Whether you face minor or major bouts of anxiety, these Biblical strategies will help you overcome the bondage of worry.

7 Powerful Strategies to Break the Chains of Anxiety

1. **Don't condemn yourself.** Accept your struggle but try not to dwell on it. Don't add to the burden of fear with self-condemnation. Turn your attention to recognize the cause. Anxiety has a root fear or unmet need.

2. **Dig beneath your feelings to discover what you believe in the moment.** Many of our emotional beliefs are related to meeting core needs for love, value, security, and acceptance. Feelings harden into beliefs when we allow emotions to become bearers of truth. Identify the root of fear rather than try to beat the symptoms. As with many emotions, worry can reveal what we believe in the moment.

3. **Surrender the right to have things work out according to your plan.** As long as you insist on your desires, you

will resist what God is doing through your challenge. Surrender is a test of faith that holds the keys to freedom. "Trust in the Lord with all your heart and do not lean on your own understanding. In all your ways acknowledge Him, and He will make your paths straight" (Proverbs 3:5-6).

4. **Choose to trust God in spite of your feelings.** "And we know that God causes all things to work together for good to those who love God, to those who are called according to His purpose" (Romans 8:28).

5. **Pursue comfort and strength in Scripture.** Meditate on Bible verses to encourage your heart. "If I should say, 'My foot has slipped,' your lovingkindness, O LORD, will hold me up. When my anxious thoughts multiply within me, your consolations delight my soul" (Psalm 94:18-20).

6. **Understand God sometimes allows us to face challenges we cannot overcome on our own.** Trials often bring us to the end of our ability to solve our problems on our own. "Consider it all joy, my brethren, when you encounter various trials, knowing that the testing of your faith produces endurance. And let endurance have its perfect result, so that you may be perfect and complete, lacking in nothing" (James 1:2-4).

7. **Rely on Christ to help.** "Be strong in the Lord and in the strength of His might" (Ephesians 6:10). Ask Jesus to give you strength and peace. "Be anxious for nothing, but in everything by prayer and supplication with thanksgiving let your requests be made known to God. And the peace of God, which surpasses all comprehension, will guard your hearts and your minds in Christ Jesus" (Philippians 4:6-7).

Anxiety can hold our hearts captive with an iron grip of fear. Though we may experience fear, we can learn to break the chains of powerful emotions. Faith is for living out of the shadows of fear in the vibrancy of God.

*All Scripture verses are NASB.

Hoping for a Happy Ending
by Tessa Emily Hall

Writing a book is therapeutic for me. I enjoy weaving together the tough aspects of life into a story that brings meaning to hardships. A story that wraps up in a satisfying, happy ending.

Because that is what we yearn for in life, isn't it? We long for hope in the midst of tragic circumstances. We yearn for meaning in the midst of pain. A reminder that despite how our "story" might look right now, it will turn out all right in the end.

In my YA novel, *Purple Moon*, Selena grew up in a Christian home. She grew up believing in Jesus and that He had the perfect "fairy tale life" planned for her. But as she grew older, this hope began to diminish.

Her dad kicked her and her mom out of the house.

Selena and her mom moved from Kentucky to a cramped apartment in Brooklyn, New York.

And just like that, she went from being a kid full of hopes and dreams and laughter—to a caregiver for her now alcoholic mother.

Little by little, Selena's hope of a "fairy tale life" vanished.

Can you relate to this?

Maybe you, too, envisioned the *perfect* future for your life—one that entailed getting into the perfect college, or starting your dream business before you reached the age of thirty. Perhaps you imagined living the happily-ever-after marriage, one that was free of strife and hardships.

But over time, reality grew into focus. Those life goals transformed into simply "fantasies."

Let's face it: Life is dirty. It's messy. And no, it *doesn't* always turn out the way we imagined.

I believe it's during these seasons when the enemy tries to plant lies in our heads—ones that cloud our minds and keep us from seeing anything beyond darkness and our current situation. These lies steal our joy, zap our strength, and keep us from moving forward and into the plans God has for us. Jesus said, "I have come that they may have life, and that they may have it more abundantly" (John 10:10 NKJV).

We forget that God has given us a purpose. That He can give us the strength to keep going, and that all things can turn out for the good of those who love Him (Romans 8:28).

So how can we remind ourselves of the truth and break free from a dark state of hopelessness?

1. **Turn our thoughts toward God. Praise Him and trust Him in the midst of pain.**

    > Brothers and sisters, think about the things that are good and worthy of praise. Philippians 4:8 NCV

    By lifting our eyes to Christ, the "dirty" aspects of our lives fade from view. When we do as Scripture says and meditate on what is praiseworthy, our spirits begin to lift.

    God's light can pierce through the darkness when we praise Him in *all* circumstances (Psalm 34:1). Doing this can then enable us to view our lives from *His* perspective.

2. Remind ourselves of who God is and how He has proven Himself faithful in the past.

Scripture says that God is:

- Faithful (1 Thessalonians 5:24, Deuteronomy 7:8-9, Joshua 23:14)
- Good (Psalm 119:68, Psalm 107:1)
- Bigger than our circumstances (1 John 4:4)
- Loving (Romans 5:8, 1 John 4:7-12)
- Our Companion (James 4:8, Psalm 9:10, Matthew 28:20)
- Our Helper in any situation (Hebrews 13:6, Romans 8:31-39)

Spend time to reflect and meditate on all that God is. By reminding ourselves of how He has proven faithful in the past, we can be encouraged that He will see us through our situation once again.

3. Spend time with God.

When we spend time in God's presence, we are filled with peace, joy, and love. This can, in return, give us the strength we need to face the day (Psalm 28:7).

Our life is only a vapor (James 4:14). The *only* thing that will last is our relationship with Jesus and the work we've done to build His kingdom.

God doesn't want us to become like the Israelites and roam aimlessly around in the wilderness for years and years, unable to pull ourselves out of a hopeless state of mind.

Instead, let's choose to trust that "joy comes in the morning" (Psalm 30:5 NKJV), despite how dark the night appears. Let's choose to lift our eyes beyond the wilderness—past our current circumstances—and see to the "land" beyond.

But even more than that: **Let's grow closer to God during these hardships and find fulfillment not through circumstances, but through Christ alone.** Because ultimately, our hope shouldn't lie in the illusion of "perfect circumstances" on earth.

Rather, it should rest in the promise of our eternal, problem-overcoming life with Christ.

And *that* is our hope of a happy ending.

Easing the Gnaw of Loneliness
by Katy Kauffman

The hunger finds us at opportune times—when we're alone at night, when we hear that friends are hanging out, when a relationship has ended. A craving to be with people starts to nibble at our hearts, and sometimes it can be satisfied with a phone call, a visit to Facebook, or a prayer. But if we can't satisfy the hunger for fellowship soon, the gnaw of loneliness can eat away at our peace and joy. Have you felt it?

No one is immune. Single people, married people, the young, the more seasoned. It finds us. Satan likes to use loneliness as a choice weapon to steal our joy, peace, and hope.

Two women in the Bible could have given in to the gnaw of loneliness and resided in its pain. One woman, Naomi, was well on her way to getting there, but the other woman, Ruth, clung to hope. She actually clung to Naomi, and in doing that, clung to God. After both of their husbands had died, Naomi told Ruth, her daughter-in-law, to go back to her own people and their gods. But Ruth chose to stay with Naomi and follow her God. Ruth's beautiful words to Naomi were:

> **"Entreat me not to leave you,**
> **or to turn back from following after you;**
> **for wherever you go, I will go;**
> **and wherever you lodge, I will lodge;**
> **your people shall be my people,**
> **and your God, my God.**

> **Where you die, I will die,**
> **and there will I be buried.**
> **The LORD do so to me, and more also,**
> **if anything but death parts you and me"**
> **(Ruth 1:16-17 NKJV).**

Ruth loved Naomi, and her commitment to her took her to a new place, the land of Judah, Naomi's homeland. As she faithfully worked in the fields to have food for herself and Naomi, she caught the eye of the landowner, Boaz, a relative of Naomi. Ruth's loyalty to Naomi and her honorable character moved Boaz to protect Ruth and give her access to his fields. He took care of her, and eventually gave her a home and a family. Naomi gained a son-in-law and later a grandson. God took care of both women, and their sorrow and loneliness ended.

If you're going through a season of loneliness right now, don't lose hope. Cling to God, and do the work you know to do to take care of yourself and those entrusted to your charge. Trust God to provide what you need. He knows how to bring the season of loneliness to an end and to ease its gnawing ache. If we try to satisfy our need for fellowship and companionship our way, the results could cause more harm than good. But if we trust God to meet our need, we not only get what He can provide, we get *Him*.

The Strategies

Here are some strategies for easing the gnaw of loneliness and replacing it with hope, peace, and joy.

1.   Talk to the Friend who is always present with you.

> God is a Friend who never leaves us nor forsakes us (Hebrews 13:5, Proverbs 18:24), and He never gets tired of us talking to Him. Tell Him how you feel, focus on His goodness, and ask Him for what your heart needs. Also, take time to hear from Him.

2. **In down times (when you're not around people), cherish the times you did have with them recently, and trust God that He'll provide more fellowship opportunities.**

    Remember the positive times with people that God has provided, and use the solitude for good—have a quiet time, clean the house, catch up on your to-do list, or send someone an encouraging e-mail.

3. **Be the initiator.**

    We can wait for people to befriend us or to check on us first, but if we like for others to do that for us, let's do it for them! Some of my best friendships started because I was willing to talk to the other person first.

4. **Remember that other people feel the gnaw of loneliness, too.**

    Don't let Satan fool you that you're the only one. Pray for friends who struggle with loneliness, and seek them out—visit them, call them, or send them a text or a care package in the mail to show them that you love them and are thinking of them.

5. **Don't let a need for companionship drive you to get ahead of God and make bad decisions.**

    This is what Satan wants us to do. He knows that we can damage good relationships and future ones by trying to meet a need our own way instead of God's. Before you visit a questionable website, push God's boundaries on romance, or give in to a feeling of hopelessness, appeal to God for help and direction. Don't put yourself in a position that will make the loneliness and pain worse instead of easing it. Meeting needs our own way can bring misery, sorrow, and pain; but meeting needs God's way brings joy, peace, and blessing.

6.   Rule your emotions, instead of letting them rule you.

This is a tough one for me. It's so easy to drown in negative feelings, but in Christ, we have the power to rise above them. God helps us to replace harmful emotions with good ones. Depend on God to choose hope instead of despair, joy instead of sorrow, and helping others instead of drowning in personal pain or loneliness.

This is *your* life. You decide what rules your spirit. Let God rule your spirit with power, love, and a sound mind (2 Timothy 1:7). Let Him strengthen your heart with His joy, hope, and goodness. Refuse a "victim" mentality, and look at all the good things God has given you. Cling to the promises of His Word, and trust Him to provide what you need. Let that faith bring you peace and joy.

7.   Cling to God.

This is the first thing that we should do, but I wanted to save the best for last! Like Ruth clung to Naomi, cling to God. Through bouts of loneliness over the last couple of years, I learned how to practice this, and the fellowship I had with God sustained me and chased away feelings of loneliness. The gnaw was eased, and closeness to God filled my heart with love and peace. But I found that drawing close to God and staying with Him in my perspectives and mindset, needed to happen every day. Cling to God daily, and remember that He's holding onto you.

If you're in a season of loneliness, turn this season into good by deepening your relationship with God like never before. The closeness you develop with Him will sustain you now and in the future. God will become your center of gravity and keep your heart anchored in hope and joy, no matter who comes or goes in your life. He knows how to make you stronger through the trial and to sustain that strength when the trial ends.

Disarming Enslaving Thoughts
by Katy Kauffman

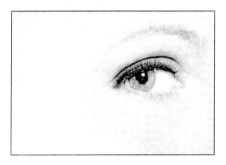

The mind is a constant battlefield. Satan knows that if he bombards us with negative thoughts, they are likely to influence how we live. He wants to steal our peace, rob us of our impact for God's kingdom, and send us into a tailspin of mental bondage and emotional turmoil.

Enslaving thoughts used to frighten me. As a teenager, I wanted to honor God in my mind, so when I heard bad words on TV or in movies, I was paranoid about remembering them later. Later in life, I allowed a certain way of thinking to dominate my thoughts, and I experienced a barrage of attacks from the enemy. I felt like there was no way out. I couldn't escape my own mind, and although I knew God was powerful enough to free me, I couldn't figure out what I needed to do.

But God was faithful. He knew how to rescue me. By His grace, I was able to overcome the spiritual attacks that Satan sent in the form of enslaving thoughts. The way out? To bury my head and heart in Scripture. I took time to look at God's Word and to make notes about what struggles people in the Bible went through, what God did to help them have victory, and what they needed to do. God helped me to apply that to my own life, and after six months of mental turmoil, I was free. God was gracious and I turned my notes into a blog series, and eventually into a book, *Faith, Courage, and Victory*. Oh, the wonderful grace of God!

I don't know if you're experiencing a barrage of negative thoughts right now, but perhaps you have in the past. It can be crippling. We can't escape our own minds. Thankfully, Satan can't read our thoughts, but he can certainly send harassing ones. However, the God whom we love and serve is greater than any spiritual attack, and the Lord to whom we belong has more authority and power than all of Satan's evil forces combined.

> **"For though we walk in the flesh,**
> **we do not war according to the flesh.**
> **For the weapons of our warfare are not carnal**
> **but mighty in God for pulling down strongholds,**
> **casting down arguments and every high thing**
> **that exalts itself against the knowledge of God,**
> **bringing every thought into captivity**
> **to the obedience of Christ."**
> **2 Corinthians 10:3-5 NKJV**

Instead of our thoughts holding us captive, we can take them captive and bring them before the King of kings and Lord of lords. If they don't match His honorable character, His darkness-piercing truth, or His matchless love, we can reject them in His name. Satan doesn't get to have any place in our minds, hearts, or lives. They are home only to Christ and His glorious truth and perfect love. Anything that falls short of that, must flee.

The Strategies

When you are tempted to let a negative thought enslave you, try practicing the strategies on the next two pages. If you're caught in bondage to a wrong way of thinking, have faith in God that you can get out. Victory is possible because God makes it possible. But you have to want it and do what's necessary to get it. Bury your head and heart in Scripture, and see the reality you have in Christ and the restoration that's possible when we turn to God for help. Freedom is ours if we practice what God has taught us in His Word and if we fill our minds with thoughts of God, His truth, and His amazing love.

Practice these strategies to disarm negative thoughts and break free from them.

1. **Identify the source of the thoughts.**

   What started the wrong way of thinking? Understanding the source of our misery is the first step to overcoming it. Did the thoughts come from Satan, criticism, social media, a TV show, or a negative experience? Ask God for help in dealing with the thoughts and to limit your exposure to what's stirring them up.

2. **Don't feel guilty if negative thoughts come to mind.**

   Sometimes you can't control what thoughts come to mind, but you can control what to do with them. See #3.

3. **Refuse thoughts at the door of your mind.**

   You hold the power of filtering what your mind dwells on. When an enslaving thought comes knocking, don't open the door. Keep the door of your mind locked against everything that will damage how you see yourself in Christ, how you view God, how you relate to others, and what you do for God and His kingdom. Your mind directs your life. Keep your mind locked up against negative thoughts and open to God and His ways.

4. **Flood your mind with good things.**

   You can't focus on two things at once. Displace enslaving thoughts with a flood of freeing ones. Keep a journal of positive, liberating Bible verses, and memorize them! When a thought comes knocking, see if it matches the truth of God's Word, and if it doesn't, quote a Scripture verse (or read it) to counteract the negative thought.

   You can also keep a journal of things you're grateful for. Be active in a Sunday School or Bible study group that discusses God's Word and shares what God is doing in the members' lives. Focus on good things, so there is less room for the bad stuff.

5.   Tap into the power of music to hush negative thoughts.

When a loved one was in the hospital last year, I was able to calm distressing thoughts by singing *Broken Vessels (Amazing Grace)*. The melody and the words calmed my heart and mind, and I was able to focus on God and His power to help my family member. Silence negative thoughts by singing songs that focus on God and His power. Praise Him for who He is, and watch Him calm the turmoil within.

6.   Disarm lies with the truth.

Refuse lies from Satan by holding fast to the truth of God. Know Scripture for yourself so you don't let Satan's lies steal your joy, zest for life, confidence in God, and belief in your own self-worth.

7.   Align your heart and mind with God's.

The best way to change how we think is to ask God's help in aligning our desires, goals, and thinking to His. He is sane, He is sound, He is peace. Drawing close to Him chases away the forces that keep us captive in wrong ways of thinking. He defeats our spiritual enemies, heals past hurts, protects our minds from current attacks, and makes us whole on the inside. He fills us with a love that satisfies our hearts, and He renews our minds with the truth. He is the answer to our bondage, and He is always willing to rescue us if we turn to Him.

Learn to think in the patterns of Scripture, and let your desires and pursuits match God's will for you. The peace will come back, and the "sanity" will return.

Pride's Dirty Little Trick
by Josie Siler

Pride has a dirty little trick up its sleeve.

Sneaky. That's what it is. It's a sneaky little beast that is hard to kill, especially when we're unaware of its existence!

Pride can start out good. We can be proud of ourselves for overcoming a fear. We can take pride in a job well done. We can even be proud of resisting sin. These things aren't sin in and of themselves. So where does the danger lie?

The danger lies in taking things too far, getting in too deep. And that's where pride's dirty little trick comes in. The sin of pride slowly sneaks into good things and before we know it we find ourselves in the bondage of sin. We may look pretty on the outside, but inside we're bound and bruised.

What does sinful pride look like?

The dream was so vivid that when I woke up, I wasn't sure what was happening. Once I collected my senses, I immediately repented. Now, you probably think I'm crazy for repenting for a dream, but it was that sneaky little beast of pride that I had to repent of.

In my dream I was speaking with a group of young girls about something. It was a good conversation until pride reared its ugly head. I heard myself stating a fact about how I have led my life. Now, there was nothing inherently wrong with what I said. It was the truth. The problem was in *how* I said it. My words were dripping with sinful pride.

I awoke with a start and knew it wasn't just about the dream. I struggle with pride. It's my downfall. I think that many "good Christian" guys and gals secretly struggle with pride. We're proud that we're "good" and haven't committed any of those "big sins" like adultery or murder.

When I woke up, I told God that I was sorry for being prideful and thanked Him for His forgiveness, because the truth is that what I was proud of in my dream, I'm proud of in real life too. Sinfully proud.

Sinful pride can sneak into our lives so easily, but it doesn't have to stay.

How can we overcome sinful pride?

Remember our sin.

I know this sounds a little, I don't know, morbid, but it's important to remember that even if we don't commit the "big sins," we do sin. In God's eyes, sin is sin. Romans 3:22b-23 (NKJV*) says, "For there is no difference; for all have sinned and fall short of the glory of God." I'm not saying that we should dwell on our sin, but we should remember that we do sin and fall short of God's glory every day. It's hard to remain prideful when we're confronted with our sin.

Remember God's gift.

Romans 6:23 reminds us that, "The wages of sin is death, but the gift of God is eternal life in Christ Jesus our Lord." When we remember that Jesus went to the cross and died for our sins, pride falls away. Everything that we have, everything that we are, is because of God's gift of salvation. Remember God's gift.

Read God's Word.

All it takes is a few minutes in God's Word to remind us of our sin and God's grace. Hebrews 4:12 says, "For the word of God is living and powerful, and sharper than any two-edged sword, piercing even to the division of soul and spirit, and of joints and marrow, and is a discerner of the thoughts and intents of the heart." If we ever wonder if our intentions are pure, if our pride has turned sinful, all we have to do is spend time with God in His Word and He'll let us know the intents of our heart.

Give God Glory.

When pride sneaks in, we claim glory for ourselves. The most important thing we can do to combat pride is to give God glory. Acknowledge that any good thing you are, have, or have done (or haven't done) is by the grace of God and His good favor. Knowing that will lead you to praise God for what *HE* has done. Deuteronomy 10:21 reminds us that "He is your praise, and He is your God, who has done for you these great and awesome things which your eyes have seen." Glory belongs to God, not us.

By remembering our sin, remembering God's gift, reading God's Word, and giving God glory, you will be able to overcome pride and send that sneaky little beast packing!

*All Scripture verses are NKJV.

Breaking Free from Unforgiveness
by Leigh Powers

Loving your enemies sounds easy until you have one. Early in our ministry my husband and I had to deal with an individual who slandered us and sought to do us harm. Walking through the process of forgiveness was tough, but it was also necessary. The cost of not forgiving is our emotional and spiritual health. Unforgiveness leads to spiritual bondage.

How the Bondage Begins

Unforgiveness begins with a hurt or offense that we can't or won't let go. We may do this for different reasons. Sometimes a hurt is so deep that it's easier to hold onto the pain instead of doing the deep work of soul-healing. Sometimes an offense hits the trigger of a past hurt, and we emotionally respond to the past as much as the present moment. Unforgiveness begins when we cling to the pain rather than moving through forgiveness into freedom.

How Unforgiveness Affects Our Lives

Jesus tells us to forgive for our own benefit. Forgiveness opens up our souls so Christ can come in and heal. Unforgiveness keeps us locked within a self-made prison as bitterness slowly poisons our souls.

Unforgiveness produces:

- **Bitterness.** If a thorn or splinter punctures our skin and can't be removed, sometimes our bodies respond by building up scar tissue around the intruder. The same thing can happen with our souls. Without the healing process of forgiveness, the splinters of hurt and anger work their way into our hearts. We surround these soul-splinters with the scar tissue of anger, hate, and resentment. Eventually this bitterness becomes evident and poisons our other relationships—not just the one impacted by our unforgiveness.

- **Lies that become our reality.** One of the dangers of unforgiveness is that in times of conflict we sometimes internalize false beliefs about ourselves, other people, or God. A child who grows up with a critical parent may come to believe he will never do anything right and is always destined to fail. A girl whose friends betray her may decide people are always going to let her down. A victim of violence may wonder why God wasn't there to stop it and determine she has to depend on her own abilities to protect herself from now on.

   Our beliefs determine our realities. If you believe your friends are always going to betray you, you constantly live with that expectation. Minor conflicts become an excuse to hurt them before they hurt you and a reason to be the first one to walk away. Believing you can't do anything right becomes a self-fulfilling prophecy and a reason not to try. Part of the process of forgiveness is getting God's perspective on our situation and replacing Satan's lies with God's truth.

- **Isolation and Further Wounding.** No one likes being hurt. If you burn your hand on the stove, you're likely to be more careful cooking so you don't injure yourself again. When we're hurt in a relationship, a common response is to be more cautious in other relationships. This can produce isolation and further wounding. Relationships require trust, and it's hard to build that trust when you keep the world at arm's length. Forgiveness helps us keep our boundaries permeable—keeping out that which would harm us but still allowing in what helps us grow.

Overcoming Unforgiveness

There are three things I think are essential to overcoming unforgiveness.

1. **Recognize the truth about forgiveness.** Sometimes we are reluctant to forgive because we harbor misconceptions about forgiveness.

    *   Forgiveness doesn't mean what happened wasn't wrong or didn't matter. If it wasn't wrong or didn't hurt, there wouldn't be anything to forgive.

    *   Forgiveness doesn't mean going back to the relationship and letting yourself be hurt again. Forgiveness and reconciliation are two separate things. Wisdom may dictate putting new boundaries in place as a part of the process of forgiveness. Forgiveness is free. Trust and respect are earned.

    *   Forgiveness doesn't depend on the other person's repentance. Forgiveness is between us and God— something we do for our own soul's healing. Part of the process of forgiveness is stepping back and trusting God to deal justly with those who have hurt us. When we forgive others, we set our own souls free.

2. **Understand that forgiveness is a spiritual task.** One of the reasons we struggle to forgive is that we try to do it in our own power. We know we're supposed to forgive, so we grit our teeth, gather up our courage, and try—only to get frustrated when we can't let go. Forgiveness is a spiritual task accomplished by the Spirit's strength. We are able to forgive by relying on God's power, not our own.

3. **Walk through the process of forgiveness**. We talk a lot about our need to forgive, but we don't always spell out well how we are to forgive. I see five basic steps in forgiveness:

   - Acknowledge the pain.
   - Invite Jesus in to heal.
   - Ask God to help us see this situation and this person as He does.
   - Relinquish our right to revenge, and trust God to deal justly with the situation.
   - Pray blessings over the person who has hurt us.[1]

   We may have to walk through this process in layers, but I find these steps helpful in dealing with my own need to forgive.

Forgiveness can be tough, but it's also essential. If you have struggled with unforgiveness, there is hope. Christ is our great soul-healer. Turn to Him and ask God to give you the strength to forgive.

[1] For more detail on these steps, see the free e-book I offer to subscribers at my blog, http://leighpowers.com.

Escaping the Rut of Bad Habits
by Katy Kauffman

Bad habits are like deep ruts in the road that are difficult to escape. As we navigate our way through life, we may find ourselves caught in one. Ruts can ruin our godliness, our relationships, and our spiritual health and strength. They can damage our joy, peace, and even our sanity. The more we say yes to these bad habits, the deeper the rut becomes. So how can we break free?

Strategies for Escaping a Bad Habit

1. **Recognize the bad habit for what it is—not a help but a poison.**

   We often start a bad habit to fulfill a need or to solve a problem. But inevitably bad habits do us more harm than good. Satan's lie is that we can exchange God's way of doing things for harmful habits and they won't hurt us. But we end up poisoning our minds, hearts, relationships, and often our bodies.

2. **Identify why you started the habit in the first place.**

   What need was the habit supposed to fill, ease, or silence? Get to the root of the problem, and don't be afraid to talk to a trusted friend or counselor about what's going on. Talking through things may help you find the root cause of the habit and give you a basis to break free from it.

3. **Find out what God's Word says about how He can meet your specific need.**

   Satan's counterfeit is a cheap substitute for God's best. God cherishes His children and knows how to provide for our every need (Matthew 6:32, Romans 8:32, Philippians 4:19). His timing and method may not be what we expect, but what He can give is so much greater than what we can try to scrounge up on our own.

   Search the Bible for the words *need(s)* and *desire(s)*. What does it say about God meeting our needs and the desires of our hearts? What does God's Word say about the root need that spurs the bad habit? Hold on to God's promises and truths, both the truths that comfort and the truths that warn.

4. **Depend on God to take care of you and to help you stop practicing what hurts you.**

   You're not alone in the fight to break free (Philippians 4:13, Hebrews 13:5, Psalm 18:39a). You have the most powerful and loving Person available to help you. So look to God, depend on His strength, follow His prescriptions for freedom, and stay under His protection and blessing.

5. **Practice the principle of displacement—displace the bad habit with good ones.**

   If you put your fist in a glass of water, what happens? The water comes out. If you start practicing good habits, there won't be as much room for bad ones. Displace the bad habit with healthy ones—listen to more Christian music that focuses on God, maintain a regular quiet time, spend time with family and friends instead of pursuing the bad habit, do fun things with good people, start a hobby you've always wanted to do, listen to good sermons on the way to work or as you pick up the kids from school. Choose those habits of mind, heart, and life that keep your focus on God, your faith in Him strong, and your mind centered on good, healthy things.

6. **Transfer the emotional fulfillment that you gained from the habit to your relationship with God and the good things He has given you.**

A habit can become an emotional crutch—that's why it's so hard to break. Find your peace, joy, and energizing strength in God and the blessings He's given you. When you see the habit as a poison instead of an emotional fulfillment, the emotional appeal grows less and less. The joy and strength God gives are lasting, but the emotional boost a bad habit gives, is temporary. That's why we have to repeat the habit to be happy, and we end up damaging ourselves.

7. **We're not likely to fix a bad habit overnight, so keep trying until you succeed.**

Don't beat yourself up with guilt if you slip back into the bad habit. God knows how weak we can be, but in Him we can be strong. So stay close to God and depend on Him to break the bad habit. Ask Him for forgiveness when you slip, and then get up and take the next step on His path. Getting up when we stumble is just as important as choosing to break the bad habit.

8. **Remember *why* you're stopping the bad habit.**

Choose Godly habits for the good of your soul, the well-being of those around you, the depth of your relationship with God, the freedom and healing you need, and your effectiveness for God's kingdom. It's not easy, but it's worth your sanity and spiritual health and strength. And very often, your emotional and physical health too.

God has helped me to stop harmful habits. Trusting Him has brought me peace and joy. I trust Him that He will meet my needs and guide me through life. I have peace that He will provide what I need in just the right timing. The joy of life with Him has sustained me, and He has provided people to walk with me through life, people who are trusting Him, too.

Cast off the chains that bind you to fear, worry, frustration, and bad habits. Escape the rut. Embrace those godly habits that contribute good to your life. The process isn't easy, but it's worth every ounce of fight you have in you. And you don't fight alone.

Overcoming Legalism
by Katy Kauffman

Racing in a potato sack is awkward. Any burst of energy and a zeal to win must be harnessed, because if you try to run at all in a potato sack ... *splat*. Down you go.

At Field Day in elementary school, I learned what it felt like to move hindered. Bound. It wasn't possible to run free like the wind. If I moved forward, I had to hold the potato sack at my waist and hop. And if I fell, I went down confined in my sack. Claustrophobic. I couldn't wait to get out of that sack.

When we hold on to legalism, we move through life hindered. Bound. Our hearts may find security in adhering to rules, but we miss out on the freedom of focusing on a relationship with God. When we operate in life like God intended His children to, we can run like the wind.

Why Legalism May Be Appealing

Legalism can become an oppressing bondage in the lives of believers, but some of us have a tendency to run toward it. Although we were saved by faith, we may try to keep a good standing with God by keeping His rules as well as our own. Rules apart from relationship. Maybe we were taught that obeying the rules keeps you safe, keeps you walking on the straight and narrow. Maybe we turned from a wild lifestyle and found relief in a set of dos and don'ts. But if we practice legalism, we miss out on resting in the unconditional love of God who cherishes us regardless of how good we are. Yes, God blesses us when we obey Him, but God's love for us isn't dependent on our performance. He loves us because that's who He is—He *is* love (1 John 4:8). In this we find freedom.

Learning to Run Well

> "You ran well.
> Who hindered you from obeying the truth?"
> Galatians 5:7 NKJV

If legalism is trying to hinder your race, hold on to the truth. We were saved by faith, and that's how we continue the Christian life. Our faith and cooperation with God, along with His work, make us holy. The "rules" or principles that He gave us in His Word, help us to become more godly, but they don't give us eternal life. Faith is key, and for the daily Christian life, so is love.

God wants us to obey Him, not out of a sense of duty (*I have to*), but out of love (*I want to*). Bask in the freedom of God's love for you, and focus on your relationship with Him, rather than on dos and don'ts. Let His love motivate you to practice His ways. Your soul will gain some breathing room, and you won't beat yourself up when you mess up. I know because I've been there.

5 Strategies for Overcoming Legalism

1. **Remember how your relationship with God began.**

    How did you receive eternal life—by doing good works or by receiving God's grace? Rest in the fact that God saved you because you trusted in Jesus. Salvation is His work in us, and God doesn't leave us on our own to live the Christian life. He is still working to make us like Christ, as we cooperate with Him.

2. **Make your primary life's goal to know and love God.**

    This is what God wants most—for us to know and love Him (John 17:3, Mark 12:30). He is all about relationships.

Sharing life with Him and helping others to know Him is life's greatest adventure. Don't make your goal of life to never mess up or to keep a rigid set of dos and don'ts. Return to the joy of your salvation—fellowship with God and His people (1 John 1:3, 7).

3. **Obey God because you want to, not because you have to or because you're scared not to.**

Let a love for God motivate you to walk in His ways. He is so good, so loving and kind, so patient with us. He knows when to get our attention and discipline us, but He is longsuffering. His perfect love for us doesn't change, so let that love be an inspiration to follow Him.

Set aside "duty" to walk in a vibrant, warmhearted, close relationship with God. Consequences for disobedience can motivate us to be good, but we may decide we can handle them and choose against God's ways. I've found that loving God is the strongest motivation for obeying Him. We fight for what we love, and we live for what we love.

4. **Fall in the arms of your loving, heavenly Father when you mess up.**

God knows that His children battle a sinful nature, and the battle is tough. But He has given us the Holy Spirit to help us win that fight (Galatians 5:16). As our sympathetic High Priest, Jesus helps us to walk on God's path for our lives, and He intercedes for us (Hebrews 4:15, 7:25). When you mess up, don't run from God, but run to Him. "If we confess our sins, He is faithful and just to forgive us our sins and to cleanse us from all unrighteousness" (1 John 1:9 NKJV). Run to God when you mess up, repent of the sin, and keep moving forward in life with Him.

5. **Have grace toward others when they make mistakes.**

When you allow yourself some breathing room to make mistakes, you will give breathing room to others. The grace and forgiveness that we have received from God is an example of how to forgive other people (Colossians 3:13). Since God has been gracious to us in our failings, we can show the same kind of love to others.

If you've seen legalism attempt to hinder your spiritual race, may God help you to throw off the chains of "duty apart from love" and to run your race well. He wants you to run unhindered.

Don't Be a Mad Monkey
on a Light Pole
by Ron Gallagher

Among the many things that the 2016 contentious political season revealed is the uniquely bipartisan nature of anger. Voters were angry, politicians were angry, party leaders were angry, and even pundits and news commentators were angry.

A recent news story about rescuing an escaped chimpanzee fits in perfectly. It followed a report about a political rally featuring clips of angry people inside an arena making speeches, while a crowd of angry protesters outside were holding signs, chanting, and shouting their disapproval of everything supported by the people inside. Next up, the chimp—screaming from the top of a power pole, showing his teeth, waving his arms, and shaking his head. I couldn't help but wonder, "Now, is he a Republican outsider, or a liberal Democrat?"

Anger's an interesting phenomenon. When I think about anger, memories of fictional characters come to mind. I see Rocky Balboa's face being pummeled into a bloody pulp by Apollo Creed as Pauly and Mick look on. "He's getting killed," somebody says. "No," Pauly answers excitedly, "he's gettin' mad!" Then Rocky begins to unleash a devastating attack on Apollo's midsection. It's as though Rocky is OK for Apollo to beat him in the head for three or four rounds, but eventually it starts to get really irritating, and once that happens, it's a whole new world.

Other fictional characters, from "The Incredible Hulk" to "The Tasmanian Devil" to "Popeye the Sailor" have cashed in on the idea. Anger has consequences, and when it shows up, people change—some to the degree that the Myers-Briggs Personality Inventory folks would have to invent a whole new section. In any case, it's an area that God takes special interest in, because some of our lives seem to be controlled by it, instead of the other way around.

It may be arguable that Jonah's recent experiences had given him reason to be irritable, but God didn't give him a pass on it, and decided to give him a lesson or two in anger management. The problem emerged in connection with the astounding exhibition of repentance and faith in Nineveh following Jonah's preaching. It was a spiritual awakening of historic proportions, and instead of praising God for it, Jonah sulked in anger.

The account of his response is brief and to the point. "But it displeased Jonah exceedingly, and he became angry" (Jonah 4:1 NKJV). The Hebrew makes it clear that he wasn't just mildly upset, either. Jonah was infuriated, and declared to God that the kind of response going on in Nineveh was exactly why he didn't want to go there in the first place. The outpouring of God's mercy and grace on them, was not what Jonah wanted to see, because they were unspeakably evil and didn't deserve it.

When Jonah didn't get his way, he went off into the hills to pout. God miraculously caused a large plant to grow up so that Jonah would have shade from the sun's oppressive heat. With the arrival of the plant, Jonah took some time off from whining. The KJV describes Jonah as "exceeding glad" for the plant (Jonah 4:6b), and the NASB says he was "extremely happy." To say the least, Jonah got a major uptick on his attitude meter and became the antithesis of his former self.

Then God sent a voracious worm to feast on Jonah's newfound little "happy bush." He followed that by turning up the heat even more, and blowing some scorching wind Jonah's way. It's not hard to feel a bit sorry for the guy, in spite of his petulant response to the joy going on down in Nineveh, but we need to pay attention to the lesson, because it isn't just about Jonah. Some of the rest of us have a hard time dealing with life when things don't go our way.

Like pressure that builds prior to a volcanic eruption, there is always some kind of pain underlying and preceding our anger, pain that demands to be expressed. Whether it stems from physical distress, relational betrayal, some kind of oppression, spiritual frustration, or something else, pain brings the message it always brings, "Something isn't right—do something to fix it." Pain and anger's instinctive response is to take over management of the whole system. Its preference is to declare its message by lashing out to replicate itself in those seen as its cause. Allowing anything that powerful to take over can blind us, and disrupt God's purpose for both us and the emotion He built into us.

God asked Jonah, "Is it right for you to be angry?" (Jonah 4:4 NKJV). He might well have added, "Does it fulfill My purpose, or only cater to the impulses of your fallen nature?" Jonah's response might have felt easy and natural, but it led him to impulsively hand the reins of an emotion loaded with energy over to people and circumstances beyond his control. He yielded to its power and blamed others for the consequences.

When Jonah hiked up to the mountains, he only elevated his physical point of view, not his spiritual perspective. The energy in anger is powerful. It can consume and shackle us altogether, and the question God chose to ask Jonah is appropriate when anger arrives and we're confronted with our natural inclinations—"Is it right?" Am I looking at this from God's perspective? Is what I'm doing, thinking, or planning what He would have me do? Is my response going to alleviate the pain, or simply multiply it? After all, a monkey on a light pole can be angry and make a spectacle of himself, but it doesn't accomplish much.

The Art of Staying Positive
by Erin Elizabeth Austin

Judgmental. Harsh. Critical. As Christians, we are taught that we shouldn't be negative in our outlook on life. We're supposed to be happy, positive people who always see the glass as half full, but that's easier said than done. Personally, it's something I only manage to accomplish when I regularly ask God for help.

Whether or not we like to admit it, I think most of us have the tendency to be a little cynical in the way we view what's happening in the world around us. Because there is so much evil in the world, we're taught that we shouldn't trust others. As children, we learn not to talk to strangers. As adults, we're reminded not to pick up hitchhikers on the street. We're even taught as we grow up to stay away from people who dress a certain way because as a general rule that means they're bad. And while it's good to exercise caution in this day and age, I can't help but wonder if we've become too critical and narrow-minded.

I'll never forget the first time I learned this truth. When I was in the eighth grade, my youth group went on a weeklong mission trip to Washington, D.C. We worked on the two roughest, most crime-ridden blocks in the whole city, and I left the city a changed person. All my life, I had been taught to be wary of homeless people. They were most likely drug addicts who were homeless because of their bad choices, and they were reaping the consequences of their mistakes. Yet after a week of working in a homeless shelter, I was shocked and appalled by how wrong I had been.

Yes, I did meet drug addicts and alcoholics, but I also met orphans, street children, and entire families who were homeless through no fault of their own. I'll never forget the man who lived and worked in the shelter for six months. He had been diagnosed with a chronic illness, and became too sick to work. Because he had no family, he eventually lost his home and his car. He had nothing. Through rotten circumstances, he became homeless, and he wasn't the only one I met with a sob story.

I met children who were dressed like street urchins, but they were the sweetest kids I've ever met. The only thing they wanted was to be loved, and at one point, I had ten different children trying to sit on my lap at the same time. But I almost didn't take the opportunity to talk to these amazing people because of my preconceived notions and critical spirit.

I hate to say this, but the American church has the tendency to judge others by their outward appearance. We have cowboy churches, motorcycle churches, Baptists, Methodists, Catholics, and on and on it goes. There are churches for different races, and some based solely on the belief of how a Christian is supposed to dress. And heaven forbid someone from a different walk of life attends one of these churches! Now don't get me wrong, all churches aren't like this. I've been in a few churches filled with all races and styles of clothing, but these churches are few and far between. As a general rule, American Christians can be a critical group of people, but that's not how God intended us to be.

Matthew 7:1-2 (NLT) says, "Do not judge others, and you will not be judged. For you will be treated as you treat others. The standard you use in judging is the standard by which you will be judged." Stop and think about that for a moment. God judges us according to the way we treat others. That's a scary thought! Yes, God is a loving God, but He's also aware of how we treat others, and that includes what we think about others. It's not our job to judge others; it's God's. He's the only One who can see a person's heart. None of us are infallible. We don't know why a person acts the way they do. As believers, our only job is to be the hands and feet of Christ—nothing more and nothing less. But we can't do that if we're being critical.

I can't help but wonder what God could do through us individually and as a group of believers if we stop being so focused on making others fit into our criteria of "normal." What would happen if we begin to daily ask God to help us not be judgmental or critical and see others the way He sees them? We might just change the world.

I'm willing. Are you?

Seeing the Beauty:
One Way to Overcome Depression
by Katy Kauffman

The water was a brilliant blue and green. On my birthday last year, I visited my first New England beach. If you know me well at all, you know I love the beach. I even collect sand. Right now, my desk is littered with jars of sand, needing to find a permanent home. Every beach I remember visiting (I got started young) has made a home in my heart.

When my family discovered Nahant Beach right outside Boston, I didn't know I was going to discover the prettiest water that I ever remember seeing. Under the sun, the shallow water danced with a magical green tint, and as the shoal grew in depth, the water grew to a postcard-worthy blue. Gorgeous. It wasn't until later that I realized I needed help seeing the brilliant colors of the water.

When I took off my sunglasses for a few minutes and glanced at the water, I saw how "normal" the water looked—blue with only a tad of green visible. When I put my sunglasses back on, I could see the beauty again. The glasses cut out the sun's glare, and their brown tint enhanced the gorgeous color of the water. Without outside help, the colors were masked to my eyes, but with my sunglasses, I could see the fullness of the beauty before me.

As we walk through life, we can appreciate the beauty around us—God's creation, the fellowship of family and friends, the activities at church, and the accomplishments at work or at home. But heartaches, trials, and spiritual harassment can color how we see life and dampen our outlook. The beautiful begins to appear "normal," and the colorful shades of daily life become tainted. The weight of life's burdens can grow to the point that we become depressed, and the weight of negative feelings masks the beauty that we once appreciated.

We need God's "glasses." We need to be able to see life—with its burdens and trials—from His perspective. One way to overcome depression is to see life as God does, with its beauty and good things. Our spiritual enemy wants us to focus on our problems and what we don't have. God wants us to focus on Him and have faith that He will help us and provide for us. When we view life from God's perspective, we can once again see the beauty that He has put in our lives, and we can remember all the good things that give us joy and strength.

So are you wearing God's sunglasses? If you're going through some spiritual depression right now, search His Word for good promises that you can hold on to, and ask Him to help you to see your life from His vantage point. What good is God working in your life? How do your family and friends bless you? What good gifts has God given? How can you give what's good to others? When we shift our focus from burdens to God, we have reason to flourish in joy, and we have motivation to share the goodness of God with others. He makes life beautiful and worth living.

Nine Ways to Overcome Depression
by Katy Kauffman

A nagging at the heart. A heavy fog. A stabbing pain. Although spiritual depression comes in different forms, its effects are usually the same—lost zeal and sense of purpose, subdued energy, sadness, a weakened desire to do routine things, and even doubts about our usefulness to God and His plan.

Identify the Source

Whether I have sudden feelings of depression or they come on so gradually I don't notice till I'm caught in a "fog," I have to identify the cause of the depression. Sometimes it's a prolonged, personal struggle. Sometimes it's Satan trying to hinder me from living for God and serving Him. But as long as I don't identify what's going on, the fog, the nagging, the pain—it continues.

We're Made to Be Overcomers

As new creations in Christ, God's children are made to be overcomers. "Yet in all these things we are more than conquerors through Him who loved us" (Romans 8:37 NKJV). With Christ's help, we can win the spiritual battles that plague us.

So let's break free. Since Christ has set us free from a yoke of bondage to sin and other spiritual bondage (Galatians 5:1), let's not allow anything to keep our hearts imprisoned, including depression. Some depression is caused by a chemical imbalance in the brain, and can be treated by medication. And should be. Other depression is caused by spiritual forces, external circumstances, or how we respond to sources of agitation, and with God's help, we can overcome it!

The next time spiritual depression tries to imprison your heart in a perpetual state of gloom, try implementing these ways to break free. God hasn't left His children without armor (Ephesians 6:11-18), defenses (Psalm 46:1), and strategies to be overcomers.

9 Ways to Overcome Depression

1. Ask God to help you identify the source of the depression and have His wisdom to know how to deal with it.

2. Remember to see life and its circumstances from God's perspective, and remember the good things that He is to you and has given you.

3. Say no to the "wolf" by depending on God's power to refuse Satan's tactics in your life.

4. Choose who you're going to be—a victim of problems and circumstances beyond your control or a victor in Christ who rises above problems and walks with God in power.

5. Trust God that He has a good plan for your life and the lives of those you care about.

6. Hold on to the promises of God's Word, and continually fill your mind with its truths.

7. Don't be so focused on what's wrong that you miss the miracles God wants to work every day—the good things He does that only *He* can do. He works good out of evil and mends the brokenhearted.

8. Remember there are people and valuable things (like love, truth, and justice) in this world that are worth fighting for.

9. Remember you're not alone in battling depression and other people need help too—maybe even those closest to you.

This is your life. Your precious life. Don't let depression steal your joy and energy. Don't let Satan hinder your adventures with God. I know from experience that we can rarely "snap out of" depression. We have to fight our way out. And every inch of progress toward victory, is worth the struggle. After all, God has more joys and adventures waiting to be discovered. Let's overcome depression and be a part of them.

Fight Indifference
with a Flame of Love
by Laura W. Watts

As we hung the last pair of jeans on the clothes line, my sister whispered in my ear, "Guess what? We're going to the beach next week." I jumped up and down with such excitement I got tangled in the wet clothes and fell backward into the empty basket. As a young child, I had a vibrant passion for life and adventure. I loved, cared about, and found joy in the simplest of things.

Somewhere along the road to adulthood, excitement took a detour. I traded high school friends for marriage and motherhood, and my dream of world travel retreated to the scrapbook. Then, divorce shattered my world, and my zeal for life dwindled to exhaustion. In pain and bitterness, I built a wall around my heart, never to be hurt again. But, the wall worked in both directions and prevented love from flowing out to anyone other than my son. Before long, I became indifferent.

"The tragedy of love is indifference." - William Somerset Maugham

8 Symptoms of Indifference:

- Fears commitments
- Hides the heart in a vault
- Walks by the homeless man and avoids eye contact
- Donates to the local food pantry, but never meets the

needy families

- Does nothing for the vast suffering around the world, because the problem is too big
- Drives past litter along the roadside every day, but never stops to pick it up
- Attends church and pays tithes, but doesn't share the Gospel
- Stares at the cross of Christ with tearless eyes

The chains of indifference slither around our hearts with every hurt and pain we experience. Without healing, these build up and impact our attitudes and actions. We don't realize we're entangled by indifference until life takes a sudden turn, and we feel the tug of chains pulling against us.

Breaking Free

1. **Realize that the chains of indifference may stem from various causes.**

   One common source is broken relationships within the family. Another cause is disappointments with the church which can drive a believer out of fellowship for years. The most difficult step forward is learning how to trust again, and in our human strength, this seems impossible. But be encouraged—there's hope for healing the wounds of broken trust, because God gives His children the ability to trust again.

   "For nothing will be impossible with God."
   Luke 1:37 NASB

2. **Search for the key to unlock the chains.**

   Talking with someone opens the door for healing to begin. Find a trusted friend, or seek a counselor through a local church. If you are experiencing severe depression and apathy, be sure to talk with your doctor. Prayer is free to everyone, and God, our Creator, wants us to come to Him for help.

"I sought the LORD, and he heard me,
and delivered me from all my fears."
Psalm 34:4 KJV

3. Take a step outside the comfort zone.

Look around your neighborhood for someone who needs a helping hand, or find a community outreach event such as a food drive for the local food pantry. Start small and try different approaches until you find one which suits you the best. Remaining in the chains of indifference is not an option, especially for children of God. Living in neutral doesn't reflect God's love to the world.

"In the same way, let your good deeds shine out for all
to see, so that everyone will praise your heavenly Father."
Matthew 5:16 NLT

4. Feed your mind with new thoughts.

The Word of God and His promises renew our minds with truth we can depend upon. Begin reading God's Word, and write down verses for encouragement and strength. Speak truth aloud daily to remind yourself of how much Jesus loves us.

- God gave His only Son to die for me, so I could live. (John 3:16)
- Jesus gives me light to take away my darkness. (John 8:12)
- The Lord loves me and takes care of my every need. (Psalm 23)
- Jesus will never leave me. (Matthew 28: 20)
- The Holy Spirit is my counselor. (John 14:16)

"The entrance of Your words gives light;
it gives understanding to the simple."
Psalm 119:130 NKJV

5.   Open your heart to love.

When we open the door of our hearts to God, His love comes in like a flood, and we can't keep it to ourselves. He gives us more than we need, because we are His vessels to carry His love to others. As symbolized by the cross, God's love flows in two directions—from God to us and from us to others. Without love for God and others, there is no true knowledge of God.

> "Love means doing what God has commanded us,
> and he has commanded us to love one another,
> just as you heard from the beginning."
> 2 John 1:6 NLT

6.   Spend some time at the cross.

Meditate on Jesus and His passion for mankind. When Jesus left His glory in heaven, He knew He would face death on the cross to rescue a dying, lost world. Wait there at the foot of the cross until you come face to face with the Lamb of God. Open your heart to the unquenchable flame of compassion. Allow His blood to touch your heart and ignite a fire within.

> "Who is it that overcomes the world?
> Only the one who believes that Jesus is the Son of God."
> 1 John 5:5 NIV

God's love set me free and sparked a flame of love that burns brightly in my heart again. Pray for the Holy Spirit to fill you with the fervent love and power found only through the cross of Christ, for this is the power to break the bondage of indifference.

Taste and See the Good:
A Weapon against Complaints
by Lauren Craft

The cold wind tore through me like a train at full speed. Rain soaked my hair and water droplets clouded my glasses. Busy professionals walked by carrying umbrellas, but I didn't have one that morning. Eight more blocks stretched between me and my office.

As I pulled my jacket closer, I knew I had a choice. I could allow my discomfort to remind me of everything not-so-perfect in my life, letting a complaining spirit drain me before the workday had even begun. Or, I could fight off the temptation, wielding a grateful heart as my weapon. God's Word urges us to rejoice always, no matter the circumstances. This was an opportunity to give that wisdom a fair chance, despite how impossible it seemed.

Walking farther, my eyes drifted to a flower bed I passed on the edge of the sidewalk. Each blossom had started as a tiny seed, which knew just how to grow into the colorful, delicate plants in front of me. So small, yet so impossible for humans to copy. My thoughts stayed fixed on this little miracle. When I stepped up to the threshold of my office, wringing water out of my hair, I was grinning.

The root word of "rejoice" is "joy." Rejoicing adds seasoning to even the worst days, placing an extra gleam in our eye. Our culture, though, is wired for negativity. When one friend asks,

"How are things with you?" the other often responds, "Going well, but ..." We focus on the "but" and ignore the blessings. Whether we complain silently or to others, it may offer momentary relief but then leaves us with hollowness, robbing us of God-given joy.

What if we have a good reason to complain though? Many of life's hardships cut much deeper than a cold, rainy walk. Jobs end and loved ones die. Spouses disappoint us and friends hurt us. Some weeks, it's the little problems that hurt because so many pile up at once. Whatever the situation, pain takes time to process, and Scripture urges us to seek godly advice. God isn't dismissive of these sufferings: "The eyes of the LORD are on the righteous, and His ears are open to their cry" (Psalm 34:15 NKJV*). Crying out when we suffer isn't the problem. When we let complaints blind us to the gifts of God, when we give problems more attention than they deserve—that's when we tie ourselves in spiritual bondage.

David faced many trying times. He walked into battle against Goliath without a sword, he lost a son after begging God to spare the boy, and he felt the stab of betrayal more than once. Still, David knew how to stop a complaining spirit from digging deep roots. In Psalm 34:8, David said, "Taste and see that the LORD is good." Tasting is more than smelling or touching. It means savoring wholeheartedly, absorbing something so close that it becomes a part of us. Many of David's psalms inspire us to be better "rejoicers" by tasting God's gifts. These are just a few of His treasures:

- The thoughtful way our bodies are crafted. "I will praise You, for I am fearfully and wonderfully made" (Psalm 139:14).

- God's forgiving, merciful heart. "As far as the east is from the west, so far has He removed our transgressions from us" (Psalm 103:12).

- The miracles on display in nature. "The heavens declare the glory of God; and the firmament [sky] shows His handiwork" (Psalm 19:1).

- God's character lessons, which shape us more into His likeness. "The humble He guides in justice, and the humble He teaches His way" (Psalm 25:9).

A grateful spirit like David's is freeing, erasing negative thoughts that blur our vision. When the picture is clear and sharp, we see that our blessings far outweigh any reasons to complain. We are made in God's image, gifted with unique abilities, and sent with a purpose. His followers are loved, forgiven, redeemed, and destined for an eternal home beyond the boundaries of our imagination. Even a hardship can be used as spiritual training, if we take full advantage of the opportunity.

Fixing our eyes on the good also makes us more like our loving God. He sees past our faults, looking ahead to the creation He hopes to mold. We can try our best to do the same with the days God has given us. The next time a complaining spirit threatens to restrain you, write David's words in Psalm 118:24 across your heart: "This is the day the LORD has made; we will rejoice and be glad in it." Whatever the day brings, it is a gift from God, waiting to be opened, tasted, and cherished.

*All Scripture verses are NKJV.

Disarming Prejudice
by Katy Kauffman

December. I thought it was a unique name. Before I went with my church group to inner city Memphis, I had never met a girl with that name. That night our group joined forces with a church to share the gospel in their neighborhood and to have an evening VBS. Their members didn't share the same color "tent" as we did. They were black, and we were white.

The kids were so joyful. I knew inner cities had their share of problems, and since we were visiting the inner city at night, I was a little worried. But this church was bright inside, not just from its lights, but from the light that shone from the people's faces. The kids smiled at us and the adults greeted us as we entered their church. I was probably thirteen years old or younger at the time, and I didn't have too many friends who had a different skin color. The fears and stereotypes that stemmed from news reports were disarmed that night.

A girl named December and a congregation who loved Jesus— they were like me. They loved God and wanted other people to know Him. Their joy and hospitality still remind me that people are people. Souls don't have a skin color. Traveling the world has shown me that people everywhere have the same need for God and His Word and the same desire to be loved.

Prejudice is an ugly monster that can be fueled by fear, misunderstandings, ignorance, and generational perspectives. Depending on where you grew up, you may not have seen much prejudice, but in recent years, the media has shown that this monster still lives in our country. And it is deadly.

When a person who is supposed to protect others does the opposite, fear grows. When a citizen takes matters into his own hands and attacks innocent people, anger develops. Some prejudice can be remedied with the truth—God has created all people equal. Other prejudice will be remedied when both sides live by what God says is right. May the gospel remind us that we all need God and we are all loved by Him. May God's love unite our country and extinguish hate and anger.

Even if prejudice is not something you struggle with, consider praying these strategies for the areas of America that still reel from prejudice's hurtful vendettas. The loving, wise, prayerful, law-abiding citizens of our nation can work together to disarm prejudice and give each other reasons to be trusting and hopeful. Respect, honor, and justice start with each of us choosing God's ways of thinking, feeling, and acting.

5 Strategies for Disarming Prejudice

1. Get to know someone who has a different skin color.

This is the simplest way to dissolve unfounded fears and to banish ignorance. Meeting December and having friends who don't share my skin color have shown me that we have so much in common. It has taught me that we think alike and that we want the same things out of life.

I won't forget the missionary from Haiti who poured out her heart to me about her life story and the many girls in her orphanage. I will cherish the memory of a Brazilian college student who helped me to overcome my fear of sharing the gospel and translated my words as I told second graders about God and His love. I still laugh at the funny stories that my teenage friend told me about her father who scared her at night from beneath the catwalk in their house, saying her name in his deep, foreboding voice.

2. **Disarm lies with the truth of God—He created all souls with equal value and dignity.**

We all are made in the image of Almighty God (Genesis 1:26). We all have personalities, feelings, dreams, choices, and responsibilities. We are all of the *human* race. God knew each of us before we were born and He fashioned us Himself (Psalm 139:13-16). Each person is a treasure whose worth is priceless. When it comes to human beings, "less than" is not in God's vocabulary.

3. **Embrace compassion instead of meanness.**

The Good Samaritan in Jesus' parable didn't let cultural differences keep him from helping someone who desperately needed it (Luke 10:25-37). Although two religious leaders passed by a man who had been beaten and was bleeding on the side of the road, the Samaritan stopped. And he was the one who was always the object of prejudice!

When someone looks differently than we do, we can put ourselves in their shoes and have empathy, not prejudice. How would we want to be treated if we were in their place? When we need empathy, we don't want our skin color to get in the way of compassion.

4. **Look for ways to build bridges.**

Simple acts of kindness can show that we have God's love for one another and that we belong to Him (John 13:35). I love seeing pictures on social media of policemen spending time with children (black or white) and laughing with them. Those kids are likely to grow up seeing policemen as trustworthy. I once read a story on Facebook of a black mother who took her son to the park and stopped to ask a policeman if she could pray for him. Acts of love like these can bridge a gulf of mistrust and build sound relationships.

5. **When you have reason to be afraid, put your trust in God and do the good you know to do.**

Maybe the area in which we live is subject to prejudice, fear, and violence. In those places, we can ask God for help and protection as we go about our daily lives, and do the good He has told us in His Word to do. We can see people (really see them), care about them, show respect, pray, give, use wisdom and caution, and pray some more. Doing "good" can create such a shockwave that eventually everyone in our city may feel it.

One way to promote unity is by joining forces with other people who are like-minded to cover your city with prayer and good deeds. Ask other churches to join yours to host a VBS or block party. Create a joint Christmas concert and pageant. Seek God's guidance to make a difference, and trust Him for the results.

People are people. They laugh, they cry, they hurt, they have victories. We all need God, His Word, and His love. What part will you have in healing divides and disarming prejudice where you are? Will you join me in covering our country with prayer and living for God so that prejudice finds no home in any of our hearts? People are precious. With wisdom and love, we can live like they are.

Overcoming a Rebellious Spirit
by Katy Kauffman

Like most young men, he ached for adventure. Independence. Freedom to live as he wanted. The prodigal son got what he wanted—his portion of his father's money and the freedom to pursue whatever he desired.

Dreams morphed into nightmares when the money ran out, his friends deserted him, and he craved the slop that he fed to the pigs. His rebellious spirit brought him low, and there was none to help. Or so he thought. (See Luke 15:11-24).

A rebellious spirit whispers lies to get what it wants. *No one will see. This won't hurt anyone. The consequences won't be too bad.* We nurture a rebellious spirit when we buy into its lies, throw off wisdom, and dive into what we know isn't good for us. We either don't stop to think about the consequences, or we decide our way is worth it. We set aside God's commands in favor of pleasing ourselves or meeting our needs according to our wisdom and efforts.

The father in Jesus' parable never forgot about his son, and neither does God forget us. God sits on the porch, waiting for His wayward child to come home. The commands that He has given us were never meant to keep us from fun, joy, and adventure. They actually provide it. And if God's timing isn't the same as ours for receiving something we need or want, we can trust Him that He has a good reason. He loves us, and He wants us to love Him. Part of love is obedience.

**"For this is the love of God, that we keep His commandments.
And His commandments are not burdensome."
1 John 5:3 NKJV**

God's commandments will seem burdensome to a heart that is
bent on self-destruction. God's ways will seem like joy and freedom
to the soul who either trusts God's wisdom or has suffered the
nightmare of rebellion.

God gave me a warning that if I insisted on something, it
wouldn't turn out well. I didn't listen and I wish I had. My mental
rebellion created a nightmare, but God graciously restored me to
the right way of thinking. God is always willing to take us back if
we run to Him. And truly, when we turn to Him for help, He is
the One running to us.

One of the hardest things to live through, is watching a loved
one go through the consequences of rebellion. Charles Stanley
once taught that we can pray for other people, but they have to
want to receive the blessing. If someone is insisting on their way
and it's hurting them, we may want to jump in and fix things.
Perhaps, fix them! But we can't see all that God is doing to fix
things. One of His methods of restoration is to allow us to go
through the consequences of our own choices. That may be the
only way we realize we don't want our way anymore and we turn
back to God and His ways.

So open your eyes. If your loved one is going through a period
of rebellion, look for how God is working. Pray, and pray hard.
Seek God's wisdom to know how to help, and remember that God
is the One that breaks the chains. Even thick ones. (That's His
specialty.) But the one in bondage has to want to be free.

If you're the one struggling with a spirit of rebellion, open
your eyes to the consequences. Are they worth it? Search Scripture
for examples of how a person's choices cost them immensely. The
books of 1 and 2 Samuel, 1 and 2 Kings, and Judges are good
sources for those real life stories.

Make a list of all the "good" things that could come out of insisting on what you want, and then make a list of everything and everyone you'll hurt if you stay on that path. Who are the people closest to you? How will this affect them? What will you miss out on? What will they?

Then do a heart check. Often our emotions are the driving force behind our rebellion. What emotional attachment do you have to the rebellious act that draws you to it? Then ask yourself, "How can God meet this need? How can He solve this problem? What does He want for me?" He wants the best for you, for each of us. But we have to say yes. Setting aside our own way in favor of God's ways opens heaven's floodgates of joy, adventure, and blessing.

Do we want what we can get out of life, or what God can make of it? I know my answer. What's yours?

Shattering the Reflection
of a Low Self-Image
by Trina Dofflemyer

A little gang of middle school girls strolled into the powder room between classes and formed a straight line in front of the mirror to primp.

"Susie, your high cheekbones are just perfect for blush. Oh? Your great-great-grandmother was an Indian princess?"

"Linda, your waistline is so teeny tiny! I wish I was your size."

Then, my supposedly best friend said, "Trina, your face would be just about perfect if it wasn't for your nose." She didn't stop there. "It's just too big. See how wide it is here," as she pointed on the glass at my reflection.

I was dumbfounded. Crushed. I was petrified to go back into class—after all, everyone would be staring at my nose! Every time I looked into the mirror after that day, my eyes went straight to my nose. Everywhere I went, I would feel people staring at me and could hear them saying to themselves, "Wow, that girl sure does have a big nose … it's just too wide." My self-image became fractured. I was looking at my reflection in the world's looking glass.

As we grow up, we can't help but notice that our physical, intellectual, and cultural characteristics are different from those around us. If we use the world as our mirror, it will evaluate us according to its own standards, and we will see a distorted reflection of our self-image.

Somewhere out there is this conception of the ideal human being, but no one has actually ever seen this person. And yet, we all get compared to it. Society considers success to be measured by what we *are* and by what we have *done*: our physique, skill set, family heritage, education, and career achievements. Satan likes to lure us into looking at our reflection in the mirror of the world …

I haven't won any awards in my career … I'm a failure.
I'll never be as skinny and toned as she is … my body type is all wrong.
Why did I have to be born into this family?

But what do we see when we look at ourselves in the mirror of God's eyes? King David worshiped God and said,

> For You formed my inward parts;
> You covered me in my mother's womb.
> I will praise You, for I am fearfully and wonderfully made;
> Marvelous are Your works,
> And that my soul knows very well.
> My frame was not hidden from You,
> When I was made in secret,
> And skillfully wrought in the lowest parts of the earth.
> Your eyes saw my substance, being yet unformed.
> (Psalm 139:13-16 NKJV)

God designed and wove our being while in the womb. He calls us wonderful, marvelous, and skillfully created. He made each one of us with great care and an everlasting and eternal love. God doesn't make mistakes; we all turned out just like He planned. If you are feeling worthless, incapable, or significantly flawed, turn away from the world and gaze intently into God's eyes to see your true reflection.

The Strategies

Here are some strategies for freeing yourself from the spiritual bondage of a low self-image and seeing yourself in the reflection of God's eyes.

1. **Remember the truth. What someone says about you or how someone treats you may be more of a reflection of who they are, than who you are.** If someone called you names while you were growing up or your schoolmates insulted your intelligence, that doesn't make it true or right, and it doesn't have to affect your self-image.

2. **Use social media as a resource, not a mirror.** If an article begins with a guilt-inducing title, avoid it. No one can live up to an article that leads off with, "If you don't do these fifty things every day, you'll never be successful."

3. **Pray and talk to God about any areas of your self-image that you feel are fractured.** He's listening with compassion.

4. **Transform your thinking.** Replace thoughts of "I'm defective" with "I'm wonderfully created." Focus on the things you've got going for you. Remember you ARE wonderfully created, and you have contributions to make in life. This will take practice, so don't be too hard on yourself if it takes some time.

5. **Thank God for making you just the way you are** whether it's your gender, cultural heritage, family dynamics, physical characteristics, or talents. Ask Him to help you make the most of who you are. Trust His wisdom and love.

6. **Stop comparing yourself with others.** Second Corinthians 10:12 (NKJV) tells us, "For we dare not class ourselves or compare ourselves with those who commend themselves. But they, measuring themselves by

themselves, and comparing themselves among themselves, are not wise."

7. **Remember that everyone struggles with his or her self-image.** Encourage others for their gifts or traits that are important in God's eyes, if not the world's.

Culture holds up an outward ideal and says, "You must become like this in order to be accepted, desirable, and happy." On the other hand, God is whispering softly, "You are remarkable and unique. I knit you together in love. You are my beautiful creation." See yourself through your Creator's eyes and shatter the reflection of a low self-image.

Whose mirror are you looking into to see your reflection? The world's, or God's?

Christ Pleasing
Versus People Pleasing
by Adria Wilkins

Have you ever been asked to do something, and you only do it because you feel obligated? I have, but I learned years ago it is okay to say "no." Once a counselor told me I was a people pleaser. She was right. I would say "yes" to every volunteer opportunity, from teaching Sunday School to helping with the Parent Teacher Association at my daughter's school. I was left stressed and anxious because of a long "to do" list that never got smaller. All my life, I have felt this need to please everyone. I have been given some practical advice over the years, from a counselor and some friends, which has made a difference.

1. **Take a year off to rest.** At first I thought "Oh, I can't do that." It wouldn't look good if I did nothing, especially since my husband is a minister. Then I gave myself a reality check: "Why was I doing all this volunteer work?" Come to find out, it was to please people by saying yes. In the meantime, I was short with my family, tired, and having panic attacks all because of my people-pleasing tendency. So I began telling people I was taking time off. It was hard at first, but as I began to relinquish my calendar-filling duties, I began to feel a calm come over my body and mind that I never knew before. I had a newfound freedom in my life.

Galatians 1:10 (NIV*) says, "Am I now trying to win the approval of human beings, or of God? Or am I trying to please people? If I were still trying to please people, I would not be a servant of Christ." By asking this question before we commit, our answer may be different.

2. **Learn about yourself.** Take a few days to write down words that describe the person you are and things you enjoy doing. Here's what I said about myself: *firstborn, entrepreneur, mom, enjoy random acts of kindness.*

    Also, ask God to show you *new* things about yourself. Listen for His voice as you study His Word. Find a friend you can trust and ask them if they see any new areas of potential.

3. **Set boundaries.** You will be asked to volunteer, no doubt about it. Don't feel bad for saying "no." If we don't set boundaries to the things we *aren't* called to do, we'll be depleted of the energy for things God *has* called us to do.

    To help devote yourself to the right things, start by writing down your spiritual gifts. Romans 12:6-8 says, "We have different gifts, according to the grace given to each of us. If your gift is prophesying, then prophesy in accordance with your faith; if it is serving, then serve; if it is teaching, then teach; if it is to encourage, then give encouragement; if it is giving, then give generously; if it is to lead, do it diligently; if it is to show mercy, do it cheerfully."

    Besides this passage, there are many online resources available to help you determine your God-given abilities. Write down your two main spiritual gifts, then list the commitments you are currently involved in. If your tasks fall under your spiritual gifts, decide if you want to continue with these tasks. If they don't, ask yourself whether it would be best to give up that activity and let someone else do it.

Make a separate list of what you're passionate about or would eventually like to do. Dream a little here. Then, go back and see if these ideas fall under your spiritual gifts.

Ephesians 2:10 says, "For we are God's handiwork, created in Christ Jesus to do good works, which God prepared in advance for us to do."

God created us to serve Him and do good things. Let God show you the *best* areas to spend your time and talents.

4. **Please God.** I would rather hear God say "well done" when I enter heaven instead of hearing a person compliment me here on earth. We can't always have it both ways—sometimes when we focus on pleasing others, we shortchange God.

    Philippians 2:13 says, "For it is God who works in you to will and to act in order to fulfill his good purpose."

    It makes me smile to see children playing with toys or drawing a picture using their imagination. I want God to look at me in a similar way, watching what I'm doing and smiling because He's pleased.

Break the chain of pleasing people. Schedule some time this week to learn about yourself. Go to a park, coffee shop, or library with a blank journal. Make a list of every word you can think of that describes yourself. Write down your spiritual gifts and compare that to your current activities. What boundaries are you willing to set in your life to make enough time to use your spiritual gifts the way God wants you to?

The more time you spend pleasing God, the less time you will worry about the people you want to please. First Thessalonians 4:1 says, "As for other matters, brothers and sisters, we instructed you how to live in order to please God, as in fact you are living. Now we ask you and urge you in the Lord Jesus to do this more and more."

Prayer: Help me, God, to please You more and more each day I live. In Jesus' name, Amen.

*All Scripture verses are NIV.

Drawing Too Close:
Battling Lust
by Katy Kauffman

Magnets. They're fun, but they can be dangerous. My household has been home to all kinds of tools—engineering tools, jewelry-making tools, and scrapbook tools. A surprising source of pain and frustration is the magnet. The attraction between two opposing magnets is useful as a tool, but it hurts when my fingers get pinched between them.

Have you ever let your heart get pinched in a magnetic attraction? The emotional pull between a man and a woman can become so great, that getting together is hard to resist. When we allow emotional and physical attraction to override good sense, we cross boundaries that were never meant to be violated and we harm ourselves and the person we're attracted to. Lust is selfish and destructive.

The downward spiral into lust can start as an innocent desire to be close. We all want to be loved and accepted. We all want someone to care about us. If our desire for closeness isn't met in good ways, we may run headlong to the bad ones. A girl who hasn't found the love she wants from her family or friends, may try to find it in a boyfriend. A husband who is having trouble drawing close to his wife, may try to meet that need with someone else.

When a desire to be close crosses the boundaries that God has set in place, that's when we have problems. Lust is a forbidden desire. It takes what is good and distorts it and twists it, creating a restlessness within us and moving us toward a suffocating and destructive bondage. God has created boundaries concerning romance and sex for our own good, and when we crash through the fence, we initiate harm.

If you find yourself wanting to be close to someone outside of God's boundaries, consider these five lust-quenching strategies. You can win this fight with God's help, but it takes your willingness to lay aside meeting your desire your way, and limiting yourself to God's ways.

5 Strategies for Winning the Battle with Lust

1.   Flee from danger—lust is consuming and destructive.

A desire that is fed over time and ungoverned by God, grows to become a consuming, driving force in our lives. The more we say yes to lust, the more it takes over our focus, what we seek, and what we want above everything else. Even above sound reasoning.

The bondage doesn't just affect ourselves, but also those closest to us. It damages our relationships. It damages our service to God. We will hurt the person we are drawn to. The relationship that we thought would satisfy our need for closeness will turn into pain and regret, because it's a relationship that God cannot bless. He wants to give us His best, but we have to follow His prescription to receive it.

God had great plans for Samson and used him to beat back Israel's enemies. But what could Samson's life have been if he hadn't been driven by lust (Judges 16)? How much longer would he have lived, and how much more could God have used his strength to help others?

God granted Solomon the most wisdom of any man that has ever lived (besides the Lord). But yet Solomon violated the wisdom of God's word to marry 700 wives and to keep 300 concubines (1 Kings 11:3). What would have happened if he had followed God's wisdom? Then these women wouldn't have turned his heart away from God to their idols, and the kingdom wouldn't have been torn away from Solomon's son. It matters what we choose. It shows up in our lives, in our influence on others, and sometimes in the legacy we leave behind.

2. **Refuse lust on the basis of its side effects—fear, guilt, regret, haunting memories, and broken relationships.**

   - *What if we're found out?*
   - *I wish I hadn't done it.*
   - *He didn't treat me like I thought he would.*
   - *I don't know if God will forgive me.*

   Don't let these thoughts haunt you. If they already do, run back to your heavenly Father who treasures you. His arms are wide open, and His heart is always ready to forgive. Refuse to let your life become warped by lust and its side effects. Refuse lust and the pain it causes.

3. **Heed a sobering warning—God is the avenger of those who are hurt by a misuse of sex.**

   After years of participating in my church's "True Love Waits" endeavor, it wasn't until I heard my Bible study teacher talk about the subject that I had an excellent motivation for deciding true love needed to wait. She quoted 1 Thessalonians 4:3-8, and it was effective.

   > For this is the will of God, your sanctification: that you should abstain from sexual immorality; that each of you should know how to possess his own vessel in sanctification and honor, not in passion of lust, like the Gentiles who do not know God; that no one should take advantage of and defraud his brother in this matter, because **the Lord is the avenger of all such,** as we also forewarned you and testified. For God did not call us to uncleanness, but in holiness. Therefore

he who rejects this does not reject man, but God, who has also given us His Holy Spirit (1 Thessalonians 4:3-8 NKJV*, emphasis mine).

God warns us about the pain and destructiveness of sexual immorality. But if we don't heed His warnings, perhaps the strength of this warning can motivate us not to cross the line. Verse 6 says that God avenges those who are misused sexually by other people. Based on David's description of how God rescued him in Psalm 18 and defeated his enemies, I have concluded that being on the receiving end of God's avenging anger is a reality to avoid.

Don't harm—protect. Instead of inviting harm into someone else's life, seek to protect them. Decide that the pain and discipline that will come as a result of lust aren't worth the fleeting closeness you may achieve. Uphold God's boundaries as protective. He loves us so much that He gave us boundaries for our good (Deuteronomy 10:12-13). Believe that, and find in it the strength to resist lust.

4. **Believe God's counsel that indulging in sin does not bring us joy, peace, or satisfaction.**

Even though following God is often difficult because we have to battle selfishness, His ways are best. When we choose His ways, we get *Him*. The fullness of a relationship with Him. We receive the joy, peace, and satisfaction that He wants to give us if we will follow Him. And we receive the good things He gives.

- "For He satisfies the longing soul, and fills the hungry soul with goodness" (Psalm 107:9).

- "Delight yourself also in the LORD, and He shall give you the desires of your heart" (Psalm 37:4).

- "Now this is the confidence that we have in Him, that if we ask anything according to His will, He hears us" (1 John 5:14).

- "Great peace have those who love Your law, and nothing causes them to stumble" (Psalm 119:165).

5. **Set your love on God first—a burning love for God can displace the burning restlessness and drive of lust.**

We can try again and again to say no to lust because we don't want its negative consequences, and we may win the struggle. But if we say no to lust because we are convinced that God loves us and He tells us the truth concerning the dangers of lust, that assurance becomes powerful against future enticements.

If we decide that God's ways are worth choosing and we shift our allegiance to Him instead of to satisfying ourselves our way, we will win this fight. A love for God and closeness to Him will enable us to say no to the magnetic attractions that will ruin our lives and steal our joy, peace, and freedom.

When we follow God's prescription for satisfying relationships, we protect ourselves and others from harm. The waiting or self-restraint needed to do God's will, reaps so much love and closeness, it is astounding to those who receive it. Overcome lust by remembering the good and the bad. Refuse the damage it can cause and trust God for the joys that His ways bring to those who practice them.

*All Scripture verses are NKJV.

Escaping the Revolving Door of Worldliness
by Katy Kauffman

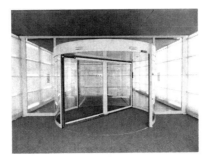

Whoosh, whoosh, whoosh. The revolving door of worldliness found me as early as kindergarten. It started when I heard girls secretly sharing who was "dating" whom, and I was disappointed that the guy I had a crush on already had a girlfriend. I jumped inside that revolving door and found myself going around in circles for years.

My thoughts centered on finding the right guy and what others thought about me—whether I dated, my looks, my clothes, and my too quiet demeanor. I wanted to look and act like the other kids, but I knew even then that God most likely had a different plan. One that was led and directed by Him, not the crowd. I realized *after* high school that people's opinions change frequently, and the one that matters most is God's.

Whoosh, whoosh, whoosh. Another door of worldliness beckoned me to enter. Ambition, prominence, and a "*Hey, look at me*" persona. I stepped inside that door for a little while, but its musty air of pride and "me-ism" grew distasteful. I realized that following God and serving Him for *His* name to be proclaimed in the world was life's purpose, not chasing self-recognition.

The world tempts us to look out only for ourselves, our dreams, and our goals. We can get caught up in advancing our careers, or even our ministries, and lose sight of what matters most—God, our families, and His purposes and ways of life. However, being convinced of the worth and greatness of God crowds out a desire to promote selfish interests, and helps us to escape the merry-go-round of me, myself, and I.

Whoosh, whoosh, whoosh. My parents keep cars for twenty years. They know how to buy cars that last, but with that comes keeping a reliable car past its "fashion" expiration date. Our reliable station wagon named "Holiday" lasted that long, and I was tempted to compare it to other people's cars. But I decided that this revolving door wasn't worth entering. We can compare our stuff to other people's stuff, but if we jump on the comparison merry-go-round, we will never get off.

There will always be someone who has a fancier car, bigger house, and cuter clothes. There will always be something we wish we had, that we don't. Yet what matters for eternity—people's souls—can't be eaten by moths or stolen by car thieves. A greater adventure than accumulating stuff, is being useful to God and being a blessing to people. It's making an eternal difference in the lifetime that is allotted to us.

Is a "Whoosh, whoosh, whoosh" revolving door of worldliness staring you down right now, beckoning you to enter? Which of its revolving doors is the most enticing to you? Although worldliness takes many forms, its bottom line is the value that is placed on self and possessing objects, versus knowing and loving people and building sound relationships.

The best door to walk through is not a revolving door of worldliness that will keep us trapped walking in circles, never getting anywhere. The best door to walk through is accepting a relationship with God by faith in Jesus, and knowing Him, loving Him, making Him known, and seeing other people discover just how wonderful He is. He teaches us what has true value in life, and He helps us to contribute value to the world.

If worldliness is trapping you in a prison of *you should have this, you should think that,* and *you should strive for this,* break free by reprogramming your value system. Spend time searching God's Word and seeing what He values, and jump out of worldliness into an eternal perspective. Ask God for how you can be about His eternal work of investing in people, and join Him on that adventure. He will open doors for you that no one can shut, and the joy and fulfillment will far outweigh anything the world could ever give you. God and His work last for eternity. Treasure what He treasures, and find your heart becoming wealthier than you ever could have imagined.

"Lay up for yourselves treasures in heaven,
where neither moth nor rust destroys
and where thieves do not break in and steal.
For where your treasure is, there your heart will be also."
Matthew 6:20-21 NKJV

The Insidious Invader
of Self-Reliance
by Jeannie Waters

It slips in as a whispering wind, transparent and seemingly good. We unwittingly welcome its arrival. At first, results are positive, triggering euphoric feelings of accomplishment and a pat on the back. "You did it!", "Good job!", and "Way to go!" echo in the brain. However, later when we stumble and fall, we identify the deception we accepted—that of self-reliance rather than trust in God.

Self-reliance doesn't surface as a dark, fear-inducing temptation, but rather as a quiet, insidious one. We can fall prey to this bondage easily when talents, intellect, or experiences appear worthy of trust. Furthermore, verbal accolades often pull us deeper into self-reliance, deceiving us into thinking we are indeed trustworthy. Masquerading as freedom, self-reliance is actually spiritual bondage which hinders victorious Christian living.

Years ago, ensnared by the self-trust trap, I became despondent. After resigning my teaching job, I visualized baking cookies, keeping an immaculate house, preparing nutritious meals, and ultimately becoming the perfect Proverbs 31 wife. One afternoon my husband's smile became a frown as I lamented, "My only accomplishments today were holding the baby and folding laundry. The clothes are still on the sofa, and there's no dinner! I can't do this!" Although my husband was supportive, my attempts to meet self-made goals with all the strength I could muster, resulted in a huge capital "F" for failure on my mental report card.

Let's turn to Scripture for God's opinion of this condition. "Whoever trusts in his own mind is a fool, but he who walks in wisdom will be delivered" (Proverbs 28:26 ESV). That verse clearly reveals God's view.

Another Biblical example is King Asa's story which exemplifies trusting God versus self-reliance. When Asa "did good and right in the sight of the LORD his God" (2 Chronicles 14:2 NASB) and led the people of Judah to seek God, he prospered as king. Later, when Asa devised his own strategies and focused on current events, peace eluded his land. Obviously, self-trust is to be avoided!

Now that we're armed with God's truth, allow me to share what self-reliance looked and felt like in my life. Then, we'll explore strategies for escaping the talons of this insidious invader and guarding against future attacks.

Suffering with the malady of self-trust, I awoke each morning glaring at a mental agenda. Anxious notions ricocheted in my brain as a steady barrage of demanding questions held me captive. "How can I possibly get all of this done today? What will happen if I don't?"

The constant bombardment of expectations escaped my grasp. Late at night I perfected my plans, and each waking hour I assessed my performance. Huge rocks of *what if*, *if I could*, and *I should have* pummeled my mind with condemnation. Laden with self-appointed responsibility, my shoulders slumped under the load.

Relying on myself felt like being stuck in a revolving door, as I laboriously trudged through life. Despite "running" rapidly, there was no escape route and no chance of progress. There was no break, no day off, no reward, no satisfaction, no time for deep breaths or naps. I was imprisoned in self-dependence, held fast by the hope I'd gain traction and live peacefully when I accomplished the next feat.

Words of Jesus freed me. "Come to Me, all who are weary and heavy-laden, and I will give you rest" (Matthew 11:28 NASB). Depending on myself had been taxing and I was weary. My Savior offered welcome relief as I confessed my self-reliance. Daily I quoted Proverbs 3:5-6 (NASB) which strengthened my resolve to place my trust in Christ: "Trust in the LORD with all your heart and do not lean on your own understanding. In all your ways acknowledge Him, and He will make your paths straight."

Strategies for Overcoming Self-Reliance

If you are exhausted from self-reliance, or if you want to guard against its insidious approach, consider these strategies and add others as God guides you to freedom.

1. **Guard your mind.**

   Certain thoughts can propel us into self-reliance. Guard your thoughts by "taking every thought captive to the obedience of Christ" (2 Corinthians 10:5 NASB). Write verses on cards to combat temptation and place them in your purse or pocket for quick access.

2. **Pray Scripture.**

   Pray Scriptural prayers throughout the day. "Let me hear Your lovingkindness in the morning; for I trust in You; teach me the way in which I should walk; for to You I lift up my soul" (Psalm 143:8 NASB).

3. **Read the Psalms.**

   Many of the Psalms teach about God's trustworthiness. Relinquish control of your life. Ask God to forgive your self-reliance and fill you with wisdom and faith.

4. **Listen to Christian music.**

   Play Christian music in the car, at home, or on a walk, thus filling your mind with God's faithfulness. Ask the Holy

Spirit to convict you of any bits of self-reliance beginning to take root in your life.

5. **Check your trust.**

Before tasks or events, ask, "Am I depending on God or myself? Who is worthy of my trust?"

6. **Transfer requests to God's Inbox.**

Write your concerns on small cards and insert them into a pretty box or basket with a lid. Acknowledge faith in God as you release the issue in prayer. Think of the container as "God's Inbox" and determine to trust Him rather than your own resources.

As a little girl, I'd hold my dad's hand, look up into his face, and delight in his smile. Our heavenly Father requires and enjoys our trust. Let's slip our hand into His, look up, and treasure the fact that He alone is worthy of our trust. Good-bye, self-reliance!

Breaking Free from "That's Just the Way I Am"
by Denise Roberts

I stood in my kitchen, tears running down my face, emotions coursing through my being, and my blood was doing the proverbial "boiling."

I have no idea what triggered this meltdown. I am sure it was a simple, silly thing that happened. But one thing piled on another, and pretty soon I was an emotional wreck, fully in bondage to the anger and every other negative emotion welling up.

I remember facing my husband and saying: "I hate when this happens. I have no control over how I feel. I don't know why I am reacting like this. I am powerless and just need a little grace coming my way from you. I am not choosing to be this way for Pete's sake!"

My sweet husband looked me in the eyes and said, "You do have a choice." Then he walked away.

Truth be told, I felt enslaved by my emotions. They certainly seemed to have mastery over me. I had become so accustomed to surrendering to my emotions that I believed that was just who I was. I couldn't change.

My husband's words were not necessarily the words I wanted to hear, but they were certainly the words I needed to hear.

As a follower of Christ I did indeed have a choice.

> Do not let sin control the way you live; do not give in to sinful desires. Do not let any part of your body become an instrument of evil to serve sin. Instead, give yourselves completely to God, **for you were dead, but now you have new life.** ... **Sin is no longer your master,** for you no longer live under the requirements of the law. **Instead, you live under the freedom of God's grace** (Romans 6:12-14 NLT, emphasis mine).

We are created as emotional beings. We are meant to feel, hurt, cry, laugh, and experience happiness and joy. Anger in and of itself is not a sin. It's what happens when we become angry that often is.

Giving in to angry, resentful, hurtful, and hurt-filled emotional responses wreaks havoc and leaves a trail of relationship wreckage in its wake. Maybe you aren't prone to an emotional, carnage-creating meltdown. But has your response to something ever been a knee-jerk angry outburst? Does the language you revert to in the heat of an argument or disagreement become "colorful"? These too are indications of being in bondage to emotional responses.

God's Word teaches us that before we are believers in Jesus for salvation we are "dead **in** our sin" (that's just the way we are), but that once we turn to Jesus and believe Him for our salvation we become "dead **to** our sin," made alive by the power of the resurrection. And the power that raised Jesus from the dead can certainly break the chains of our "that's just the way I am used to being" emotional enslavement.

How do we tap into that chain-breaking, resurrecting power?

1. Recognize and admit your "that's just the way I am" mindset. The first step in breaking the chain of emotional responses is to admit we have them. These are areas of

weakness that we seek for the strength of Christ to be infused in.

2. Commit to memory one or more verses that speak to you about being a new creation in Christ and remind you of the power available to you because you are filled with the Holy Spirit.

    "This means that anyone who belongs to Christ has become a new person. The old life is gone; a new life has begun!" (2 Corinthians 5:17 NLT).

    "God is greater than our feelings, and he knows everything" (1 John 3:20 NLT).

    "For God has not given us a spirit of fear and timidity, but of power, love, and self-discipline" (2 Timothy 1:7 NLT).

3. Recognize this is, ultimately, a spiritual battle.

    > The weapons we fight with are not the weapons of the world. On the contrary, they have divine power to demolish strongholds. We demolish arguments and every pretension that sets itself up against the knowledge of God, and we take captive every thought to make it obedient to Christ. (2 Cor 10:4-5 NIV)

    Every time we give in to the emotional outburst, the enemy wins. Choose to whom you will yield your power: your enemy or the Holy Spirit. Believe that the power that raised Christ from the dead is more than sufficient to conquer your emotional response enslavement and wrestle those old ways into conformity with who Christ says you are.

4. Dress for victory. "Finally, be strong in the Lord and in his mighty power. Put on the full armor of God, so that you can take your stand against the devil's schemes" (Ephesians 6:10-11 NIV).

5. "Always be humble and gentle. Be patient with each other, making allowance for each other's faults because of your love. Make every effort to keep yourselves united in the Spirit, binding yourselves together with peace" (Eph 4:2-3 NLT).

While there may be reasons underlying the emotional response that do need to be addressed, there is never an excuse for angry, hurtful, or offensive outbursts. Surrendering our pride softens the ground of our heart making it fertile for the Word of God to take root.

Breaking the chains of this type of emotional bondage is not an easy road. We may still yield our power to the enemy. Employing these strategies will remind us that we have the power of the Holy Spirit within us and His power is greater than the power of our enemy.

When the Pain Won't Go Away
by Katy Kauffman

Picture three women sitting at a small, round table in a busy coffee shop. As they try to catch up on the news in each other's lives and talk above the noise of the café, a quiet ache pulses in each of their hearts. An ache they can't cure, no matter how hard they try. One of them struggles with a failing marriage, the other tries to hide the incident that happened when she was sixteen, and the third never talks about the trauma she experienced as a child.

On the surface, they appear to be happy, but the ache doesn't lessen. Even with years of good memories and busy schedules, the pain seems to deepen with every passing year.

Have you been there? Is there an ache in your soul that doesn't seem to go away, no matter how hard you try to cure it? Does its pain intensify when something reminds you of its source?

When pain is birthed in our lives, it will take up residence until something greater crowds it out. For many people, getting married and raising a family is the "something greater." The demands of work and home life clamor for attention, and deadlines and busyness commandeer their time. Others set lofty goals and let ambition run its course. Still others try to find healing and peace in relationship after relationship, but the pain deepens instead of subsiding.

We can try to cram our schedules with busyness and invest ourselves in building relationships and friendships, and much of the time, pain takes a back seat. There may be little room for much else to inhabit our thoughts. Until we're alone. Or the house is quiet. Or we can't sleep at night. We need something greater— greater than our pain. We need God.

The comforting thing about God is that He sees the state of our hearts even when no one else does. He knows what caused the pain and why it continues. And He cares. No sin is too great that He turns away from helping us and offering us His grace and mercy. No trauma inflicted on us lessens our value in His eyes or causes Him to stop loving us. His fierce love for us moves Him to be our Champion. Our God does, and will, fight for us.

When the pain won't go away, let God be the something greater you need. Flood your heart with the promises of His Word. Find refuge in His massive strength and goodness. See Him turn tears into comfort, heartbreak into healing, and lost opportunities into new beginnings. Draw close to Him, and let fellowship with Him crowd out the pain. Center your life around Him and His eternal purposes—loving people, sharing the gospel, encouraging others, and doing good.

Let God heal your heart and turn your pain into a platform from which you can encourage others who are going through the same things you did. You have wise blood now. When you learn from God how to get to the other side of pain and thrive in His hope, joy, and victory, you can tell others about the Someone greater you've found.

All other "cures" have an expiration date. Eventually people get tired or busy. Church activities usually slow down in the winter. The chocolate cake in the fridge runs out, and the morning jog ends. But God never expires, He never tires, He's never too busy, He doesn't slow down, and He lasts. Forever. Find the healing you need in a close, personal, vibrant relationship with Him, and delight in the extra helps He gives you—family, friends, church, fulfilling your God-given purpose, and using the talents and gifts He has given you. Let God take up full residence in your heart, mind, and life, so that His companionship, joy, and peace crowd out the pain that doesn't belong with His unconditional love for you and the abundance of life that is yours in Christ. God is your reality now, and day by day He can lessen the pain and replace it with something beautiful.

"These things I have spoken to you,
that in Me you may have peace.
In the world you will have tribulation;
but be of good cheer, I have overcome the world."
John 16:33 NKJV

Pitching Your Tent:
What Is Your Life Centered On?
by Katy Kauffman

Some cities may be centered around a town hall or a street filled with shops and restaurants. However, before Israel had a land of their own, God centered His people around Himself.

As the Israelites traveled through the wilderness to the land of promise, they set up camp each time in the same way. Each tribe had been instructed to pitch their tents either to the north, south, east, or west, and next to a specific tribe (Numbers 2:1-34). They were all centered around one special tent—the tabernacle. The Levites were the only tribe that did not help to form a square around that place where God manifested His presence. They were to pitch their tents in the middle of the camp around the tabernacle, since they were God's special servants.

For the children of Israel, God was to be at the center of their way of life. His cloud guided them by day and His pillar of fire by night. When they reached a resting place, He was still to be the focal point. What is your life centered on? Where have you pitched your tent?

God's children today battle many distractions for their attention and many idols for their allegiance. The idol of materialism tries to claim the center spot of our camp. Or the idol of ambition. Or the idol of *me*. When we center our lives on something other than God, we will eventually find that life doesn't line up right. Our hearts aren't truly satisfied. We always need more of the idol, and we're still left restless and wanting when we get it. But when we center our lives around God, He satisfies our longing souls and fills them with goodness (Psalm 107:9). When we seek Him above all else, He lets us find Him (Jeremiah 29:13).

Idols are not as kind to us—their satisfying power eludes us, and we can end up putting a different idol in the center of our camp again and again. God is the only One who knows how to order our lives so that we find the most joy, rest in the best peace, and know the best Person. He gives us meaningful relationships and provides exactly what we need when we need it. He is a loving Father who never leaves us and who never decides that we're too much trouble or not worth loving.

Ask yourself these questions to see if you've set up camp around God and the life He has for you.

1. What do I focus on the most in a day's time?

2. What is my first thought in the morning and my last thought at night?

3. Besides paying the bills, what do I spend most of my money on?

4. What do I like to do with my free time?

5. How often do I honor God by spending time with Him, both alone and in corporate worship?

6. How often do I pray?

7. How often do I read God's Word?

8. Can other people tell that I'm a Christian by what I say and what I do?

9. How great is the strength of my love for God and for people?

10. How do I show that love in everyday life?

We can tell a lot about ourselves by looking at these things. They indicate where we've pitched our tent—close to God, or closer to the world. Close to His will for us, or closer to what selfishness dictates.

When our tent is not centered on God and not in alignment in right relationships with people, it's time to make a change. The longer we stay out of sync with God and others, the more we miss out on the joys that come from having God at the center of our lives. The more opportunities we miss out on, too.

Don't let another day pass by without evaluating where you've pitched your tent. Choose to travel through life with God at the center of it. He will give you the direction you need and people to travel with, and make the journey a life worth living. True satisfaction is found in a life centered on God and in a heart that loves Him the most.

"But seek first the kingdom of God and His righteousness,
and all these things shall be added to you."
Matthew 6:33 NKJV

Short Stories

When Fiction Is Your Teacher
by Katy Kauffman

I learn from movies, do you?

A fellowship of unlikely friends determines to destroy the ring of power. A group of children discover a magical world through a wardrobe. A girl falls through a rabbit hole and discovers she is destined to slay a jabberwocky. A CIA agent risks everything to accomplish justice.

The Lord of the Rings, *The Chronicles of Narnia*, *Alice in Wonderland* (Tim Burton's version), and the Jack Ryan series—they all taught me something about courage and life with God. When I wrestle with a bad habit or emotional turmoil, I always need to dive into God's Word and take to heart its truths, promises, and warnings. Another way that God has taught me is through word pictures—scenes from movies that illustrate spiritual truths. Such scenes have given me the extra boost I needed to live out what I knew from Scripture. Fiction has become another aid in the fight to win my spiritual battles.

This section of *Breaking the Chains* is meant to act like a series of "scenes." The short stories that follow are word pictures that illustrate spiritual struggles and victories. It's our hope that these fictional vignettes inspire you to break chains and have hope. Fiction should never replace the Bible as our teacher, but just as Jesus used stories to illustrate His points, we can use stories to aid the soul and break bondage. So dive into these stories, and take to heart the principles you see illustrated. Victory can be a reality.

The Whisperers
by Tina Yeager

Keys rattled in the outside knob. Marina gripped the kitchen counter, knuckles whitening. Her nostrils flared at the premonition of whiskey breath.

Rustles stirred in the ceiling and skittered into the walls. She suspected vermin once, but the noise resembled faint whispers more than rodent claws.

Grease leapt from the skillet onto her finger. She gasped and thrust her hand under the faucet.

Bert slammed the door and slurred. "Dinner ready yet?"

Marina's shoulders trembled. The spatula stuck midway beneath the Salisbury steak. The stubborn patty flung hot spittle onto her forearm as she hacked fervent stabs between crust and meat.

Clomp-shuffles halted at the kitchen doorway. Wisps of Bert's gel-stiffened hair unraveled onto his dewy, flushed face. The investment firm's badge hung from his disheveled tie. "Burned it, didn'tcha? Worthless—"

"Go relax. I'll have it ready in a minute." She slid the half-patty onto a chipped plate of gravy-laden potatoes.

With a shuddering inhale, she rolled her shoulders. Steadying the plate, she strode out of the kitchen.

Cigar ashes clung to Bert's Florsheims, propped on the coffee table. She inched forward, plate extended.

He snatched the dish and grabbed her hair.

A flash caught her eye. A blue skirt swished around the corner. "Cindi?" Thumps resounded up the steps. Muffled wailing ensued.

Marina jerked her hair away through his sweaty palms. "I have to check on Cindi."

"Come back here." The plate crashed against the wall. Heaving, Bert stood and gripped the couch to brace his swaying torso. He tottered and collapsed onto the cushions.

As Marina reached the staircase, the wailing intensified with dual tones. A childlike cry mingled with rasping. Her sweet baby shouldn't have to live like this.

To the right of the steps, dusky light flooded the entryway. The front door creaked and swung open.

A scream gusted in from the street. "Momma!"

The setting sun cast shadows across a hunched shape near the curb. Marina raced outside. She tore open the gate by the mailbox. It clanged behind her as she rushed to the girl's side. "Sweetie, are you okay?"

She tilted her head and rasped. "Are you?"

"Why are you in the street? I heard you scream ..." She studied her grey dress. "Weren't you wearing a blue skirt?"

"No." Her slender fingers wrapped a chill around Marina's hand and tugged her downward.

She crouched. "What is it, Baby?"

Squeezing her grip, the girl whispered, "Let's not go back in there."

Marina's eyes stung. She twisted to glance back at the house, but icy fingers grabbed her chin.

"Please, Momma."

She nodded. "I have to get some things first."

"No. Leave right now."

Thudding steps whipped her attention aside. She stood to face the neighbor as he ran toward her from the next yard. "I called 9-1-1. Everybody out safe?"

"How'd you know—" Marina glanced at the house and clapped a hand over her mouth. Ghoulish smoke wisps slithered around doors and windows. "The skillet! I forgot to turn off the cooktop."

"Where's Bert?"

"Huh?"

"Bert, and your daughter. They still inside?"

"Bert's on the sofa. But Cindi…" She glanced at the empty sidewalk to her right. "Where'd she go? She was right here."

Narrowing his eyes, he studied her face. "You were alone when I came over."

Marina dashed across the lawn, throat clinching to shred her voice. "Cindi!"

She burst across the threshold as sirens blared from the street. Smoke barged at her and dug into her lungs. She fought blind through the dense mass until her ribs jammed into the banister.

"I'm coming, Cindi!" Her knees cracked against the steps. She crawled up the staircase and across the hall. A faint ribbon of light led her to the doorway. She reached up for the knob. It resisted. Marina rammed the door with her shoulder. Pain shot through to her neck and spine. She rolled onto her back and kicked until the jamb splintered apart. Flailing, she scrambled into the room with her hands brushing across the floor.

"Please!" Her fingers swept across rubber soles and felt along them to cotton socks. The smooth, fine hairs of her little girl's leg.

A weak cough penetrated the shadows. Marina clutched and lifted the frail body to her chest. She fumbled with the sill while shifting her child's leaden weight. At last, she pried up the sash. Gagging, she tumbled through the opening. She squeezed her daughter's tender form as her shoulder scraped the asphalt shingles. A bleary glimpse of the dusky orange sky faded to black.

Darkness washed over her and receded like the ebb of a rogue wave. Bright light needled between her lashes. Beeps punctuated murmurs around her. A man and smaller figure leaned in to shade the fluorescent beams.

"Momma?" Cindi's warm, dewy palm rested atop Marina's hand. A white-stubbled gentleman wearing a suit stood behind her daughter, near the foot of the bed.

Marina raised her cord-tethered arm. Fingertips trembling, she caressed her baby's cheek. "I'm so glad you're okay."

"We can stay safe now, Momma." Cindi glanced over her shoulder.

"From fire, or … Daddy?"

She shook her head. "Neither. Something bigger."

Marina shifted her gaze from the man to Cindi. "What is it?"

"Reverend Clark says he can stop the whisperers."

"Whisperers?"

"Sometimes they look like people, even kids." Cindi nodded. "They've been around a long time. I couldn't make them go away. But he can."

Her chest drummed. Memories flashed—sinister faces and clawed wings darting around corners over the years.

Clark said, "Demons. Familiar spirits, we call them."

"Attacking Bert?" She sat up. "Is he…"

"In ICU." He bent closer. "They already had Bert. They were after you."

"But I volunteer with the prison ministry."

"Precisely. You started freeing souls without protecting yourself from their captors." He sighed. "They almost tricked you into abandoning your family in a fire you caused."

A shudder rattled Marina's core.

"Will you let him help us, Momma?"

"Long as he teaches me how to keep them gone." Marina ground her molars. "I can't abide a bully. Not anymore."

The Judge's Pit
by Rosemarie Fitzsimmons

A sliver of light from the world above crept across Deb's face, startling her awake. Rubbing her eyes, she sat up and examined her dismal surroundings.

Nothing new but the day. The same insurmountable dirt walls around her, the same brilliant light overhead, the same creep sitting just a few yards away.

Deb tugged the collar of her oversized robe closed and fastened the top button against the morning chill. She glared at her companion and spat.

"Guilty!"

Her accusation bounced from one cavern wall to another like a pinball, then careened downward, grazing her shoulder before burrowing into the ground.

"Ow!" She rubbed her shoulder and looked across the room. The creep was pouring himself some cereal, oblivious to her frustration.

"He cannot hear you, you know."

She sighed, searching the darkness of her pit in vain for the counselor, as she did every day.

"I don't know why you won't let him hear me. He deserves much worse for what he did."

This time the counselor sighed. "Deb, we've been through this. Your emotions are yours alone. You cannot pin them to anyone else. Now, how do you feel about getting out of here today?"

She eyed the beautiful opening overhead with longing and shrugged.

"I'd love to, but HE won't let me."

"The judge? Sure he will. As soon as you give him back what's his."

She patted the black velvet pleats of the robe.

"I need this. The judge doesn't understand how much that jerk hurt me."

"Deb, do you really think that's true? Have you *heard* the judge's story?"

She had, but it didn't matter. Risking another headache, she sent a scowl toward the creep, who was now whistling as he plopped into an overstuffed easy chair and flipped on the television. The scowl bounced back and stung the side of her face.

Why is he allowed to be happy?

Anger surged within her, wrapping like chains around her chest, tighter and tighter, until she could barely breathe.

"It's not the same thing!" She gasped. "This really hurts!"

As always, the counselor said nothing when she gave way to rage. She wanted him to comfort her, to tell her she was right. *Take my side, for Pete's sake.*

"Oh, precious one, I do take your side."

"I hate it when you do that. I didn't say anyth—wait. You do?"

She knew if she could see him, he'd be grinning. She always pictured him grinning, as if her life were one big puzzle and he'd spotted an important piece just under her elbow.

"I love you, Deb. Always have, always will. I want you to get out of here even more than you do."

She eyed him suspiciously.

"Then why don't you let me sentence him?" She tried to stand, but the heavy giant robe weighed her down.

"It's not my assignment, for one thing. Only the judge can do that."

"And for another?"

"For another, if you succeeded, you'd be in this prison forever."

She detested that answer, but he never gave any other. A sudden burst of laughter from the cozy chair grated against her brain like a nail on glass.

"Why must I hear *him*, then, if he can't hear me?"

"You don't have to. You choose to. This is a place of your making, not his."

Deb fingered the buttons on the robe and shouted into the darkness.

"This is all so unfair! I'm the victim here! He gets to laugh and run around while I'm chained to the ground. It makes no sense! I'm the one carrying all the pain!"

"Then put it down."

"What?" Deb scoffed, fighting the rising hysteria. "You act like I can just dump it out. What do you know about my pain?" She drew her knees to her chest and began to sob.

"Everything. More than you, believe it or not." The counselor's gentle voice stirred her heart, and she lifted her head.

"Who are you, really?"

Instead of answering, the counselor wrapped her in a soft, blanket-like hug, caressing her cheeks and rocking her until the anger waned. She melted into the warmth and murmured, "I do believe this is better than seeing you."

The counselor sang as he rocked her. After a few moments, Deb lifted her head.

"Counselor, why won't the judge come down here?"

He chuckled. "The judge won't wallow here in the darkness with you. However, he did send me. To show you the way out . . . When you're ready."

She nodded toward the laughing man in the chair.

"But why won't he take care of that?"

"Tell me something, Deb. Has he ever done anything to make you think he's not a good judge?"

Deb looked at the sky overhead. She wanted it so much.

"I guess not. It's just frustrating that he's so happy over there while I'm miserable."

"Well, you cannot do anything about his happiness. You can only control your own." She felt the caress on her face again. He was pleading now. "Deb, trust him. Give it back."

Tears flowed down Deb's face as she nodded. With shaking hands, she fumbled with the buttons at her chest. She stood and let the yards of black velvet slide off her shoulders, forming a circle on the ground around her.

"You know what you have to do, right?" The counselor held her as she filled her cheeks and exhaled deeply.

"Yes . . . I know."

Deb turned toward the man and whispered, "I forgive you. I hereby relinquish my claim to your sentencing."

The man said nothing, still glued to his television.

"I don't understand." She frowned. "He can't even hear *that?*"

The walls of her pit fell away, revealing a lovely field of roses, and she lifted her face to the warm sunshine, breathing freely for the first time in months. Before her stood the judge, beaming in his perfectly tailored velvet robe.

"My sweet Debora, of course he can't hear." He wrapped her in a loving embrace. "It was never *about* him. This was about me all along, and about you trusting me as your king."

She stepped back, her eyes wide with realization, and he laughed, pulling her again into his arms.

"Welcome back, my child. Oh, how I've missed you."

Set Free
by Evelyn Wells

Tears made tracks down my face as I stared out the school bus window. The bus lurched with every stop, and with every thrust backward, my heart fell deeper into desperation. I sent up a brief prayer, not knowing whether God heard it or not. Maybe He did, and maybe He didn't.

"Emma, would you like to have this orange?" Cathy asked. "Emma?"

I turned and saw the orange in her hand. Oh, how I wanted that orange. I was hungry.

Cathy smiled at me. "Do you want it?"

I was afraid she'd see just how much I wanted it. Cathy probably felt sorry for me, but she would never have ridiculed me. She was the nicest girl I knew.

"Thank you," was all I could manage, and I looked down so Cathy wouldn't see my tears.

I was just fourteen years old, but old enough to know I wasn't as good as the other girls at school. I'd always been told that. Not many people spoke to me, and I didn't want them to. I was ashamed. Ashamed that my mama and her boyfriend got drunk and beat me. Ashamed that I didn't have warm clothes and shoes.

I never knew much about my daddy. Mama said he left us when I was a baby; he had wanted a boy. Billy was Mama's latest boyfriend and lived with us. I didn't like the way he looked at me. I wanted to run away, but I had no place to go. All I knew was that I didn't want to live with them anymore.

The next day on the bus, Cathy invited me to her youth group at church. "Mom said you could ride with us. We go right by your house on the way."

I would have done almost anything to get away from home. Mama didn't really want me around. She told me I got in her way and was useless around the house.

"Thank you. I'd like to go to church with you. I'm sure Mama will let me."

I went with Cathy on Saturday to the youth rally. Everybody made me feel like I belonged. I went back on Sunday. And Wednesday. I didn't know who Jesus was, but as I kept going to the youth group, I wanted to learn more about Him. I started going to Sunday School with Cathy.

Mama and Billy didn't like me going to church, and sometimes I had to sneak out. They didn't believe in God, and I now realize it was because they didn't want any standards they had to live up to. They had no goals, no standards of their own. Until I began going to church, I believed I'd never amount to anything. I had been told this all my life, so it was easy to believe the enemy's lies.

Our house was empty when I arrived home from the youth group one Friday night. Mama and Billy were gone, and I never saw them again. There was no evidence of anyone ever living there. Except for the trash bag in the corner containing all my possessions.

It looked like God had been listening to my prayer after all, that day on the bus. As I walked away from our house that night, I felt like I had been rescued. After wandering around for a while, I found myself at Cathy's church.

When the church reported my situation to the authorities, I was allowed to spend the night at a church-sponsored foster home. A social worker and a policeman came to talk with me and told me that my mom and Billy had left on a bus for another state. I know I should have grieved, but all I felt was relief. I was glad they were gone. I never remembered Mama hugging me or holding me in her arms. I didn't know what would happen to me, but I didn't think it could be any worse than what I had already lived through.

The foster family in which I was placed was all I could have dreamed of. Not only was there a mom and dad, but a sister, too. She'd been adopted when she was three years old. These wonderful people formally adopted me within the year.

It didn't take long for me to learn to love and trust my new parents. Mom and Dad were so good to me, and they loved me. I could tell. It was the same with my sister. We were, and still are, best friends.

I gradually began to lose my shyness. The counselor called it low self-esteem. Since I was beginning to fit in better, I made friends with the other students in both school and church. I believed I belonged for the first time in my life.

I've heard from Mama only once since she left. Social Services contacted her regarding my adoption, needing her consent. She sent a letter, saying I was better off without her and not to contact her. My hurts were gradually replaced with forgiveness.

I was in my new home about a year when I knew I wanted Jesus in my life. I had learned a lot about Him, but I wanted to *know* Him. The happiest day of my life was when I knelt down to ask God's forgiveness and to accept Jesus as my Savior. God reached down and took away my sins, my low self-esteem, my shame, and my hurt.

When I stood at the front of the church and faced the congregation, I saw my sister, Cathy, making her way toward me with a big smile on her face. She was the first to welcome me to her church, just like she was the first to welcome me to her family.

Now I was a daughter and a sister who was loved, in my own family and in God's. Now I was set free to believe what my God and my family say about me—I belong and I am loved.

The Confrontation
by Katy Kauffman

I knew she would come, and I dreaded it. The air around me grew colder as Sibi approached. She wore her fine garments and jewels. Today I wore my armor.

But this was also the moment I had craved for so long. To be rid of her constant intrusion in my life, to silence her caustic voice, to face her and defeat her, to free myself once for all.

"I want to be free of you, Sibi, and I'm ready to fight for my freedom." I drew my sword, and its brightness flickered across her face for an instant and stunned her. Then her eyes grew dark and defiant, and she laughed.

"Do you really think you can defeat me? I've known you for too long. I know what works, and when it works. Besides, we have always wanted the same things. We think the same way. We're too much alike. You'll never be free of me."

Her taunts were close enough to the truth that I hesitated for a moment, but then I noticed my sword pulsing in my grip.

"That was true once," I told her, "but no more. I want something different, something better."

"No, you don't," she countered. She brought her hand out from the folds of her gown, and revealed her sword. Oh, how I hated that thing! It was the absence of everything good and decent, but its hollow appearance had always mesmerized me. Rather than reflecting light, it seemed to swallow it. And Sibi knew how to use it well. I still have the scars.

She lunged at me with her sword, but I stopped hers with mine. She stumbled backward from the force of it, and I advanced again. She blocked my attack and spun around to lunge at me. I heard my sword clang as it hit the floor, right before I fell to my knees. I scrambled to pick it up and protect myself.

Her strength and resolve did not fail. She struck again and again, and as she did, she reminded me of my past failures. She struck at my strength with her words, and I felt my resolve to win waning.

Then the King's words sounded in my mind, and I repeated them out loud as I swung my sword: "If anyone desires to come after Me, let him deny himself, and take up his cross daily, and follow Me" (Luke 9:23 NKJV*).

She ducked, and my aim missed her.

"Create in me a clean heart, O God, and renew a steadfast spirit within me" (Psalm 51:10).

I felt a surge of power flow to my hand. With my next blow Sibi almost lost her footing, but she recovered. I kept repeating the words of truth, and I made a commitment deep within my soul to put my trust in them and practice them.

"Walk in the Spirit, and you shall not fulfill the lust of the flesh" (Galatians 5:16).

The clang of our weapons reverberated.

"You shall love the LORD your God with all your heart, with all your soul, with all your mind, and with all your strength" (Mark 12:30).

I knocked the sword out of her hand.

"Flee also youthful lusts; but pursue righteousness, faith, love, peace with those who call on the Lord out of a pure heart" (2 Timothy 2:22).

My blow brought her to her knees, and my second thrust found its target at last. Her eyes widened in shock, and then her face softened in awe. The battle was over.

The King had helped me, and today Sibi, also known as Self, died.

*   *   *

I awoke with a start. Had it been only a dream? I hoped not. I checked my hands and knees. They were bruised and tender. Perhaps I really was free.

I got ready quickly and walked toward the school. Some of my students were arriving at the same time I was. I put my things down on the desk and asked how the students were on this Monday morning.

Then I saw her. I glanced out the window and envisioned Sibi peering at me from behind a tree. She was delighted to see my surprise. She stepped out into plain view, sat down, and arranged her fine clothes around her.

"What are you staring at?" asked one of the girls.

"Nothing," I answered. I quieted the children's chatter and asked the boy nearest me, "Do you remember the prayer that your mother prayed at your bedside the night you were so sick and we were all worried?"

When he nodded, I said, "Why don't you recite that prayer in phrases and let the rest of us repeat them after you, so we will all know it?"

The boy stood up and slowly began, "The LORD is my shepherd. I shall not want" (Psalm 23:1). We repeated it after him.

"He makes me to lie down in green pastures; He leads me beside the still waters" (Psalm 23:2).

The echo of the children's voices resonated in my ears and my spirit. I looked out at Sibi. She didn't look quite so smug.

"He restores my soul; He leads me in the paths of righteousness for His name's sake" (Psalm 23:3).

I knew what I had to do.

"Yea, though I walk through the valley of the shadow of death, I will fear no evil; for You are with me" (Psalm 23:4).

Later that afternoon, we all went outside for recess. I walked to the tree line where Sibi had been sitting. The lines of the prayer echoed in my heart. Then I knew it. One battle had been won, but more would come. I realized that defeating Self would be a daily battle, and the sword of the King and His power would be my weapons. The day I "slayed" Self became the day I learned how to win.

*All Scripture verses are NKJV.

Fight for It
by Rosemarie Fitzsimmons

Depression seeped into Mary's room like a warm, damp fog, settling onto the cozy blue blanket at the foot of her bed. She'll be here soon, he thought, and began weaving heaviness and despair into the fibers with a masterful touch. Too much, and she would notice right away. Too little, and she would not be tempted . . .

The kitchen door banged open.

"Can't anyone hear me?" Mary propped her foot against the door and tried to squeeze through the entrance with two grocery bags, a groaning book satchel, her purse, and a soaking wet umbrella.

"Sorry, Hon." Dave rushed to her side, giving her a sweet, welcoming smile. "No, I didn't hear you." He took the bags. "Bad day?"

Mary glared. "So, I'm here 30 seconds and you've already sized me up." She dropped the umbrella and bags on a chair and unbuttoned her raincoat, purposefully avoiding that increasingly familiar non-expression he put over his smile whenever she snapped at him.

Dave quietly pulled pasta, tuna, and soup from the bags, finding homes for them in the cupboards. He headed to the fridge with the hamburger and cheese. Mary wanted to start again, reverse the mood she'd established. She inhaled deeply and tried to exhale her pent-up frustration.

"I'm sorry. Yes, it was an awful day." She pulled the soup can from one cupboard and put it in another. "I didn't get the raise— what are you doing? How long have we lived here and you still don't know we have a meat drawer?"

She felt shame creep over her cheeks but couldn't stop. She snatched the hamburger from Dave's hands and shoved it into the drawer. Too proud to let Dave see her tears, Mary slammed the fridge closed and raced from the kitchen to the bedroom, slamming that door as well.

Mary fell across the bed and sobbed herself empty. The muffled television in the other room comforted her. She knew Dave was waiting. She only had to walk through the door and curl up in his lap and all would be forgiven. He'd pray with her, remind her of the good in her life, and hold her until the ugliness passed.

How did I get such a wonderful, patient man?

But she wasn't ready to talk. Mary reached down for the blue blanket and pulled it over her shoulders. The soft satin trim caressed her face, and warmth enveloped her with an understanding hug.

Perhaps a little nap.

She closed her eyes, letting the blanket draw the cold rain from her bones.

You can't work there another day. They don't like you there, anyway. You should probably quit.

Mary indulged this pitiful barrage that seeped like tiny dew drops from the blanket into her heart. She fell asleep as the subject gradually shifted.

You're a terrible wife. How long do you think he'll put up with your nonsense?

The smell of coffee permeated her senses, but Mary pulled the pillow over her head and snuggled deeper into the blanket, which had coiled itself possessively around her feet and legs.

Dave must have snuck into bed last night.

A brief regret darted through her brain. She hadn't gone to him.

Terrible, selfish wife.

The bedroom door creaked. Beneath her pillow, Mary held her breath as Dave set her coffee on the nightstand. She didn't want to see his cheerful, hopeful face. When he set a loving hand on her exposed arm, she pulled away, tucking it into the covers.

"Sweetheart, it's nearly eight. . ."

"Not going to work." She talked to the narrow slit of pant leg visible under the pillow. "Taking a sick day."

"Are you sick?"

"I'm not going to work. Would you pull the shade on your way out?"

Dave sighed as he pulled the shade and shuffled away. "I'll call in for you . . . I love you, Mary." He paused. "I miss you."

That's right. He's making this all about him.

As the door closed, Mary pulled the blanket tight. It felt heavier than it had last night.

Which is fine. Keeps the world out.

She spent the day there, getting up only when necessary, and even then remaining wrapped in her cocoon, trudging it across the floor to the bathroom and then back to bed. By the time Dave returned from work, the blanket had become so heavy she couldn't push it off. She'd pulled it across her head, and had become entombed in its protective grip.

You're never leaving. This is good. Stay here with me.

She heard Dave's footsteps nearing and cringed.

Don't lift it, don't lift it, don't—aaahhh!

Mary winced from the brightness, surprised to see the shades still drawn. Dave's loving, concerned face melted her heart, but she didn't speak.

"I can force you out of here, Mary. But you need to fight this." He kissed her forehead and set the blanket back over her, askew, before walking away.

Her arms bound, Mary couldn't reach up to close the gap he'd created. Light rushed into her prison through the sliver. She stared and heard a small plea.

Fight.

The voice hadn't come from the blanket, but from some place closer. She wanted to remember something, but the blanket pressed against her head.

Remember!

It took all her will to strain against her prison and break one arm free.

Jesus!

The light widened. She sat up, weak and dizzy. The blanket fell to her waist.

Lies. I've been listening to lies!

Mary kicked the blanket off and stood, free for the first time in what seemed like forever. She walked to the door, stronger with each step. Dave sat on the couch, head bent over his Bible. He glanced up and smiled, opening his arms.

She raced to him, finally home with his arms around her. True comfort. Real peace.

"Read to me," she said.

He cleared his throat. "You have delivered my soul from death, my eyes from tears, and my feet from falling. I will walk before the LORD in the land of the living."

Mary's eyes widened. "I believed, therefore I spoke, 'I am greatly afflicted,'" she whispered. "Psalm 116. I read that yesterday morning. I remember wondering if I'd think to call out or if I'd crumble."

Dave lifted her chin and kissed her. "You called out. So did I. That's why you're here and not still in there."

She thought of the crumpled blanket. She'd fold it later, but keep it nearby for next time.

Depression smiled, unaware that, as always, Hope waited on the pillow.

*Quoted Scripture references are Psalm 116:8-9, 10 (NKJV).

Breaking Free
and Staying Free

Comfortable in Misery
by Cherrilynn Bisbano

Don't try to fix me ... The pain goes deep.
Don't try to heal me, I'm scarred.
Your whisper echoes in my head,
"Only the Father of Light can heal."
His Word can go deep into your innermost being and search,
Search your thoughts, and heal wounds, pains, attitudes, and scars.
Is this my identity forever?
Is pain, abuse, torture, and being invisible, my identity forever?
The light is bright
The light is warm
"Hey, let go of that ... that is my identity ... how will others know me
if you take it?"
The abuse, the pain—that is how people know me.
The fear of letting go.
Do I want to be healed?
Do I want to change my identity?
The journey will be too painful.
So here I sit
In the dark,
Don't try to fix me ... The pain goes deep.

This was my life for over thirty years.

Yes, the Lord saved me at age twenty-eight. I was on fire. I memorized Scripture. I told everyone about Jesus and His healing.

However, depression engulfed me in its dark vacuum. My happy mask hid my inner angst. I was comfortable in my pain. Little did I know that my pain caused others pain.

I did not trust others and I was controlling. My bossiness drove new friends away. Fear had blinded me to the truth. I felt God's promises were for everyone else.

The Word revealed my emotional and spiritual paralysis.

> After this there was a feast of the Jews, and Jesus went up to Jerusalem. Now there is in Jerusalem by the Sheep Gate a pool, in Aramaic called Bethesda, which has five roofed colonnades. In these lay a multitude of invalids—blind, lame, and paralyzed. One man was there who had been an invalid for thirty-eight years. When Jesus saw him lying there and knew that he had already been there a long time, he said to him, "Do you want to be healed?" The sick man answered him, "Sir, I have no one to put me into the pool when the water is stirred up, and while I am going another steps down before me." Jesus said to him, "Get up, take up your bed, and walk." (John 5:1-8 ESV)

That was me! I sat on my mat for almost thirty years waiting to be rescued. I did not want to wait any longer even though my mat was safe for me. It was my identity. Each stain and raveled edge represented a part of me. I had to let go of my old identity and let the healing process begin. I was comfortable in misery, fearful of change, and too weak to do the hard work.

> Therefore, strengthen your feeble arms and weak knees. "Make level paths for your feet," so that the lame may not be disabled, but rather healed. (Hebrews 12:12-13 NIV)

I wanted to stand, walk, and maybe, just maybe, run.

The years of childhood abuse from the hands of a family member had taken its toll. My self-talk needed to change. "You won't amount to anything … you are a loser." "No one really likes you; they are just pretending."

God in His amazing love showed me the path to victory in His Word.

That, however, is not the way of life you learned when you heard about Christ and were taught in him in accordance with the truth that is in Jesus. You were taught, with regard to your former way of life, to put off your old self, which is being corrupted by its deceitful desires; to be made new in the attitude of your minds; and to put on the new self, created to be like God in true righteousness and holiness. (Ephesians 4:20-24 NIV)

God sees me as righteous and loves me. Wow, that was a concept that had never entered my mind. How could that be when I felt unlovable? I had a choice to believe the Word of the one who loves me, or to believe lies.

I not only memorized the Word, I began to apply it and put it into practice. When a voice in my head said, *You are no good,* I would speak out loud, "God loves me and nothing can separate me from that love." I would tell myself daily, "The promises of God are for me, even when I feel broken, unwanted, and unlovable."

I quoted daily, "For he chose us [ME] in him before the creation of the world to be holy and blameless in his sight. In love he predestined us [ME] for adoption to sonship through Jesus Christ, in accordance with his pleasure and will" (Ephesians 1:4-5 NIV).

He chose me. He loves me. Questions haunted me for a few years. *But what if I mess up? What if I fail Him?* I would continue to quote Scripture, "Your eyes saw my unformed body; all the days ordained for me were written in your book before one of them came to be" (Psalm 139:16 NIV).

God knew everything that I would do before I was born and still chose to save me. Wow! I could not earn my salvation, so I could not do anything to lose it. What freedom. Yes! The healing Word of God has changed this unlovable, unwanted, good-for-nothing person into a child of the Most High God.

I leap for joy as I think of how He rescued me from the dominion of Darkness and brought me into the Light. The light I once shunned. Yes, it takes work. Yes, it is hard to leave the familiar for the unknown. Yes, it's worth the angst and effort. If you are stuck on a mat, Jesus says to you today, "Do you want to get well?"

Please don't waste valuable time. Start the journey now. Jesus beckons, "Get up! Pick up your mat and walk."

Breaking Free from Hopelessness:
A Testimony
by Lorphine St Louis

Why did you have to leave? Why am I going through all of this? What did I do to deserve to be treated so harshly by my own family? Why *me*? Why, God?

These were the constant and never-ending questions that lingered in the back of my mind every waking moment. But when I was a young child faced with hopelessness, God changed that hopelessness into a life filled with hope, love, and joy through His Son Jesus Christ.

I'd like to take you on a quick journey into my dark and chilling past. I was four years old when my mother made the dramatic and unexpected decision to leave Haiti. She ran away because the man that she loved entrapped her in a life of abuse. She did what anyone might do, she ran. She ran as fast and as far away as she could to get away from that relationship.

In the 1990s, my mother risked her life by taking a boat filled with other Haitians to find safe haven in the United States. When my father realized what my mother had done, he went after her in an attempt to keep her under his oppressive authority. That left my siblings and me alone with our aunt in what would become the worst and saddest part of my life.

At the age of ten, my siblings and I were treated like house slaves. We were forced to cook, clean, and do heavy labor on a daily basis. We could not get a decent education, and we often went to bed with hunger pains. I slept on a thin twin-sized flat sheet every night on a concrete floor. My aunt often threw away food instead of giving it to us, and left us with nothing to eat for the night.

We were extremely underweight and underprivileged. I often felt like I was in a nightmare that was never-ending and impossible to wake up from. I found myself constantly asking why I had to live in this type of world. Why did this have to happen to me? Every time I saw a child with their parents, it affected me emotionally and mentally. I coveted my mom's touch, and wondered if I would ever have what that child across the street had. For me, having a parent symbolized security and love, provision and compassion, and most importantly, it meant having a relationship with someone who loved me more than life itself. That was my desire as a child—I wanted to experience love. I wanted to know that there was hope.

It was this continual desire for love and hope that led me to accept Jesus Christ as my Lord and Savior. It happened when I was eleven years old at a chapel service one day at school. I heard the speaker say that if anyone wanted to have hope, they should come forward and begin a relationship with Jesus. I remember to this day the thought that came to my mind: *If this Jesus can give me hope, I don't care who He is. I need Him in my life.*

After I gave my life to Christ at the chapel service, my aunt was unhappy with the decision that I made. She disciplined me and beat me for what I thought was the best thing that had ever happened to me. As a child, I dealt with her displeasure, but for the first time in my life, I felt joy.

It was this joy that ignited a strong desire in my heart to get baptized. I wanted to identify with Jesus through baptism, but my aunt forbade me to do it. I don't know why she didn't want me to get baptized, but I knew in my heart that I wanted to show the world that something amazing had happened to me.

I thought if I had to endure another beating to show the world how much I loved Jesus, I would do it. So I got baptized, and it was the greatest moment of my life! But when I got home, my aunt found out and beat me again, this time with an electrical plug, which left scars and bruises on both of my arms. My sister had to soak a piece of cloth in salt water to treat my wounds. However, the scars that were on my arms were nothing compared to the scars my Savior endured for me.

You see, I had joy the minute I found Jesus. My circumstances had not changed, but I didn't care about the physical pains of this world because the spiritual pain I had deep down was healed. God healed my spiritual wounds and made me His daughter! For the first time in my life, I had a Father who cared about me. A Father who promised me in His word: "Never will I leave you; never will I forsake you" (Hebrew 13:5 NIV). Jesus promised that He would not leave me as an orphan but that He would be coming to me (John 14:18). For a child who grew up without parents, that was life altering and mind blowing!

I began to realize that my past was no longer my reality. I no longer had to be held captive to the evils of my childhood and the failures of my earthly father and mother. When I placed my faith in Christ, God adopted me and set me free to experience true joy, true hope, and true love. I was no longer a slave to anything in this world.

As I grew in my walk with Christ, I realized that the earthly things that people so often desire are not bad in and of themselves. The problem is when we assume that they will bring us happiness and contentment apart from Christ. These things become diversions and barriers in our lives and ultimately keep us in bondage from experiencing the true hope of Jesus Christ. This hope that is found in the gospel, is what Jesus died to bring into this world.

Now God has blessed me with a family of my own. He rescued me and led me to a godly man that I fell in love with and married. God also blessed me with three adorable kids that I have the opportunity to love, care for, and train in the way of the Lord. We are all in Haiti serving Jesus as full-time missionaries overseeing an orphanage, a school, and a church plant that my husband is leading. God even restored my relationship with my aunt who is now a believer.

Jesus set me free and broke the chains of my house slavery, the chains of my hopelessness, and the chains of my sin. Because of Jesus, I have hope in the glorious day of His return, but as I wait, I have eternal hope now. Faith in Jesus sets us free to hope.

Breaking the Chains:
Gushing or Dynamite?
by Beebe Kauffman

Visual effects. That's what I liked best in high school chemistry class. The experiments that made a little puff of smoke, the ones that turned the smoke purple, or the ones that temporarily went awry and exploded into a little ball of fire. (The teacher always had a miniature fire extinguisher on his desk. He knew how adventurous our class members were.)

A demonstration concerning displacement involved a measuring cup, water, and a fist. Plunge your fist into a measuring cup full of water, and what happens? The water gushes out. Two things can't occupy the same space at the same time. It was a simple demonstration, but the principle stayed with me.

Our hearts and minds can be filled with what isn't good for them—fear, anxiety, selfishness, greed, and so forth—and get caught in the seemingly fixed ruts of wrong thinking and bad habits. But when we take in God's word and commit ourselves to follow Scripture's instructions and practice its wisdom, some of what is bad for us gets displaced with what is good, with what builds our spiritual health and well-being. "Displacement." Faith in the truth and faithfulness to God's ways are indispensable to it.

Faith in God's power to set us free displaces a victim mentality—I can't escape this bondage. Faith in God to understand and to offer loving wisdom for our struggles displaces helplessness.

Faith in God to stay with us through the process of gaining freedom, and to forgive us for missteps, displaces a fear of failure and its repercussions.

Faithfulness to God's ways involves putting off wrong thoughts and practices, and filling that "cup" in our lives with healthy thoughts and practices. Two things can't occupy the same space at the same time. So when we are filling our hearts and minds with Scripture, the principles of worldliness come gushing out. The wrong thoughts and practices that strengthen spiritual bondage are displaced by good thoughts and practices that strengthen freedom.

Sometimes good practices displace bad ones quietly, like the water gushing out of the cup. Other times, breaking the chains of spiritual bondage takes something more powerful.

Another demonstration involved a chemical compound that acted like miniature dynamite. The teacher used a clear glass test tube that was packed in the middle with fire-retardant "gunk." He positioned it horizontally and secured it on the lab desk. Close to the right end of the tube, a trash can was lying on its side, as if it were waiting to receive something. Then the teacher inserted a chemical mixture into the left end of the test tube, on the edge of the obstruction.

Of course all of us students were holding our breath, waiting for something amazing to happen. When nothing happened immediately, some of us looked away, wondering if the experiment was a dud. But then it happened. A little puff of smoke on the left edge of the obstruction in the tube, and most of the gunk shot out to the right, smack dab into the trash can. The chemical reaction acted on the gunk like miniature dynamite, dislodging it, and clearing out the test tube.

Sometimes our spiritual bondage seems wedged, jammed, immovable. We can't get the wrong thinking or behavior out of our lives. Our good intentions to overcome bad habits fail again. We hear inappropriate words spewing forth from our own lips, despite our earnest efforts to forsake them. Darkened patterns of thinking weaken us with fear, anxiety, pain, hopelessness, or indifference. We have lived so long with these detriments that we come to see them as a part of who we are, and they may very well be how others see us.

Then we feel remorse, regret, and frustration when we say or do, what we have pledged never again to repeat. We can feel them so often that they also seem to be a part of who we are. That's when we need spiritual dynamite—faith and faithfulness joined with two more powerful elements, a persistent pursuit of freedom and dependence on God.

A persistent pursuit of freedom is driven by dreading the costs of giving up and relishing the rewards of staying with it. We hear them from Scripture, from our pastors and Bible teachers, and from our family and friends. We hear them from our heavenly Father in quiet times and prayer. Persistence is part of the "dynamite" catalyst that helps to send the gunk that is lodged within our hearts and minds, smack dab into the trash can. It helps us to be rid of spiritual obstructions such as anger, pride, hypocrisy, prejudice, compromise, apathy, envy and others; and clears the way for us to possess relief, soundness, untainted wisdom and understanding, peace, and joy, among others.

The fourth powerful ingredient is dependence on God. When we can't break free from spiritual bondage, our job is to keep doing what we know to do, and to look to God to effect freedom. Sometimes He uses a particular experience to help us see what we haven't understood before or what hasn't registered in our minds. Sometimes He orchestrates one situation in life to give us new insight or encouragement. God works in our desires, motivations, understanding, and experiences. He builds on our faith, faithfulness, persistence, and dependence on Him, until at last the chains of spiritual bondage are broken. Then we will find that freedom is worth every bit of the investment that it takes.

"Now to Him who is able to do exceedingly abundantly above all that we ask or think, according to the power

that works in us, to Him be glory in the church by Christ Jesus
to all generations, forever and ever. Amen."
Ephesians 3:20-21 NKJV

Freedom Reinforcements
by Trina Dofflemyer

Have you ever felt elated because you were finally victorious in an area of spiritual weakness, only to find yourself spiraling back down into the same temptation the next day? We desire to be transformed, to leave habits and thought patterns and negative emotions behind. How can we strengthen ourselves for the spiritual battle that will be entailed when we step out and pursue the ways of God?

Christopher Dawson mused, "The true freedom of the world—the only freedom that can free man in the depths of his personality—depends on keeping open the channels of revelation, preserving the Word of Truth and communicating the Spirit of Life."[1] True freedom from spiritual bondage must be reinforced by continually hearing God's voice through His Word, by keeping His Word close to our hearts, and by praying to live out our lives through the power of the Holy Spirit.

Reinforcement is defined as "the action of strengthening or encouraging something."[2] When we disentangle ourselves from an area of spiritual, mental, or physical bondage, we can place reinforcements in our lives to strengthen our liberty in Christ and to encourage ourselves to be faithful to Him.

Freedom Reinforcement Number One: Transform Your Mind through Bible Study.

Sometimes we don't know we are in bondage until we study Scripture and see how God designed us to be. As our Creator, He outlines the way of life He lovingly intended for us. We learn how to live to please Him, as well as how to live a fulfilling life. We study the Bible so that we come to know God and to see how Jesus lived during His earthly life. We learn who God really is, not what we may have assumed He is like or what someone may have erroneously taught us about Him.

Studying the Bible can take several forms. One way is to be involved with a local church to hear Biblically-based preaching. We can set aside a daily time of quiet to devotionally read our Bible or use a Bible study guide. Joining a small discipleship group who is studying a particular book or topic in-depth is another option. Podcasts of sermons, Bible phone apps (some which read the Bible out loud), and online study tools are also resources. Romans 12:2 (NKJV*) tells us, "And do not be conformed to this world, but be transformed by the renewing of your mind, that you may prove what is that good and acceptable and perfect will of God." Studying the Bible will transform our thinking to the mind of Christ.

Freedom Reinforcement Number Two: Transform Your Heart by Thinking Deeply about Scripture.

We transform our hearts when we internalize God's Word. When we carry the words of God in our souls at all times, God gives us His heart for ourselves and for the world. But the ability to deeply focus is becoming a lost art in our society. We live in a culture of distraction with endless social media alerts, dings for a new text message, or a breaking news flash from somewhere in the world.

When studying the Bible, choose a verse specific to an area or habit where you are struggling for freedom. What is causing you anxiety? What spiritual or physical needs are you struggling with today? Memorize that verse (or at least try and be able to paraphrase it), and think intensely about it as you go about your day. Write it on index cards and post them around the house and in your car where you will see them throughout the day. During the commute to work, waiting in line at the coffeehouse, or while doing chores at home, you can meditate on the verse. The Holy Spirit, your Comforter and Helper, can bring it to mind whenever you need help. As Jesus did when He was tempted in the wilderness, we can use Scripture from memory to counter Satan's demonic whispers in our ear. Psalm 119:11 tells us, "Your word I have hidden in my heart, that I might not sin against You." Learning to reflect on the Word of God will transform our hearts.

Freedom Reinforcement Number Three: Transform Your Life through Prayer.

Prayer deepens our relationship with God and transforms our lives. We allow God to shape our prayers through the words we read and study in the Bible. As we think deeply about what we've read, we can pray what we have learned in order to live in the liberty Christ has purchased for us. Our heavenly Father loves us and wants to communicate with us through a close relationship.

You can pray for strength to walk in God's ways and learn to be in an attitude of prayer throughout the day. You can pray conversationally. Pray the passage you have been pondering back to God. Personalize the verse or passage. Pray for wisdom to respond to what God has shown you through the Scriptures. If you find you have no words to pray, use the prayers of Scripture. The book of Psalms is full of lament prayers as people poured out their hearts to God. Colossians 4:2 encourages us, "Continue earnestly in prayer." As we pray from our hearts, our life begins to transform to mirror the image of Christ.

When we study the Bible, our thinking is transformed in how we see God and how He created us to be. When we meditate on particular verses or passages about His ways of love, our hearts begin to change as we journey along His paths on our earthly pilgrimage. When we pray after God's heart for ourselves and for others around us, then our life will begin to reflect the image of Jesus.

The transforming grace of God allows us to take the next step to be more like Jesus, whatever that may be for each one of us. The apostle Paul tells us, "I press on, that I may lay hold of that for which Christ Jesus has also laid hold of me" (Philippians 3:12). Press on, fellow traveler, and reinforce your freedom in Christ by hearing God's voice through Scripture, keeping His Word close to your heart, and praying to live your life through the power of the Holy Spirit.

---

*All Scripture verses are NKJV.

[1] Woods, Ralph, ed. *The World Treasury of Religious Quotations* (New York: Garland, 1966), 352.

[2] https://www.merriam-webster.com/dictionary/reinforcement, accessed February 20, 2017.

Say No to the Wolf
by Katy Kauffman

I met my first wolf as a preteen visiting the city zoo in Paris, France. He was black, and I think he liked me. As I walked back and forth in front of his fenced habitat taking pictures of the wolves, he followed me. Head down. I got a kick out of this and started walking faster back and forth in front of him, hoping he would keep following me. He did. My mom called out for me to stop. I think she was wiser than I.

Not too long after that, I encountered a different wolf. As a teenager, I began having tormenting, negative thoughts. After a while, my mom realized they were coming from a spiritual enemy. They hounded me until I understood they were based on lies and I could say no to them. It worked, and that wolf left.

About fifteen years later, another wolf hounded me. In my late twenties, I experienced a spiritual battle that topped all of the others. Negative thoughts, fear, frustration, oppression, and depression. The battle (which I had brought on myself) became so severe, that it was hard to sleep, pray, or even sing praise songs. I stopped my blogging and buried myself in Scripture. I found hope there. I read about real men and women who battled darkness—whether it was Satan or their own fears or struggles. I saw what they needed to do to win the victory, and I saw what God did for them. The notes I wrote down about their stories turned into a blog series, then a Bible study to teach at church, and later a book.

Faith, Courage, and Victory is the result of God turning my hardest spiritual battle into a whole lot of good. I'm forever grateful.

Jesus taught about a certain wolf that likes to mess with God's sheep (John 10:10, 12). Satan and his forces enjoy hounding us with whatever they can use to make us afraid, lonely, distracted, frustrated, or depressed. But the spiritual forces that come against us are nothing compared to the great and mighty power of the God of the universe (Ephesians 3:20; Ephesians 6:10-13; Psalm 18:17, 27:1, 29:11, 91:14-16; Mark 1:34). Jesus, our Good Shepherd, protects and empowers His sheep. When we stay close to the Shepherd, we can count on His help to say no to the wolf that wants to make us afraid. We can refuse the spiritual depression and negative thoughts he sends our way.

If you're going through a season of spiritual depression right now, or a difficult spiritual battle, be convinced of the mighty power of God to rescue you. Your deliverance will require both God's work in your life and your cooperation. But it's possible. No wolf is bigger than God. No demon is stronger than the Lord Jesus Christ. Remember how God has helped you in the past, and trust Him to be with you now. Do what you need to do, to stop walking in front of the wolf's cage. Come away and bury yourself in Scripture, draw close to the Shepherd, and revel in the strength and joy that come with knowing our great God. Say no to the wolf, and flourish in the victory that God provides.

"Finally, my brethren, be strong in the Lord
and in the power of His might."
Ephesians 6:10 NKJV

Don't Go Back
by Katy Kauffman

Have you ever felt the relief of freedom? I have. More than once. Whether I had struggled with something for days or years, breaking out of a detrimental habit or way of thinking brought with it a wonderful conglomeration of relief, joy, and peace. Freedom can also bring restoration, renewed relationships, right values, and clear thinking.

So why do we sometimes go back? Just like the Israelites were tempted to go back to Egypt, we may be tempted to pack up and leave freedom for what has grown familiar—bondage, struggle, and defeat. That decision was made by the Israelites when they were worried about having enough food (Exodus 16:2-3). They didn't trust God to provide for them. They wanted to be slaves again rather than to trust God and flourish in the freedom He had provided.

Freedom takes work. God hasn't called us to bondage, but to be bondservants of Christ (Colossians 4:1, 12 NKJV). Jesus died to free us from sin's enslaving power, and although He has provided this reality for all who have faith in Him, we still struggle with temptation, our sinful natures, and what's "easy." It's easy to give into bondage again. It's easy to give into sin instead of fighting it and saying no. It takes work to stay free in our daily walk with God, to live as He intends for us to live—in the relief of freedom.

I once told a friend that I wondered if some struggles would stay with us all of our lives. Was there a way to break free and stay free? My friend sure hoped so. About a year or two later, I discovered the answer for myself. Yes, it is possible. And yes, it certainly takes the right focus, the power of God, daily studying His Word, fervent prayers, and two letters: no.

No, I don't want to go back to what will destroy me from the inside out.
No, I don't want to hurt my family and those I care about.
No, I don't want to miss out on God's best for my life.
No, I don't believe it's worth it to go back.

And it takes three letters: yes.

Yes, Lord, I want Your way above my own.
Yes, I care about what builds up my life and the people around me.
Yes, You're worth it. Every single time. You're worth it.
Yes, Lord, I will do whatever it takes to follow You and live free as You intended for me to live.

Walking along the beach one autumn day, I was thinking about a struggle that had plagued me for years. I decided in that beautiful place that although I could choose the right thing because I didn't want the bad consequences, I wanted the right thing because I wanted God the most. I whispered to Him, "I choose You for You." Not for just what He could give me. But for Him. To show Him I love Him, to do what I knew He wanted me to do, to please Him and honor Him.

What will you choose? At the end of this book which is full of strategies and motivations for choosing the right thing, what do you want? The relief of freedom? Sustained freedom? Then choose God for God. Because you love Him and want a close relationship with Him. Because you want to share life with Him.

Because you've seen what you—what any of us—can do in life on our own, and it's just not enough. Life doesn't work right without God. In vain we struggle for freedom if we don't depend on Him to break chains. We desperately need God for eternal life and for daily life. We need Him so that we can be free from sin's power and its eternal consequences. And we need Him so we can live victorious over sin's daily enticements and bondage.

At the close of this book, remember the articles and principles that stood out to you, and decide for yourself:

No, I don't want to go back.
And yes, I will depend on God's grace—on His ability in me—to choose the right thing.

There will be times when we have relapses. There will be stumbles or headlong falls. But our loving Father picks us up, brushes us off, and gently says, "Do you want to try again? Hold My hand, and don't fear. I've got this, and I've got you. Trust Me, and walk with Me."

Don't get overwhelmed thinking that you have to get your act together right now for the rest of your life. Choose God in this moment. Obedience is taking the next step with God. And the next and the next. It's deciding at the fork in the road that you can either do things your way or God's way, and you choose His way.

A consistent *yes* to God forms a habit, and a habit becomes a way of life. Let your yes's be more numerous than your no's, and you will find it easier to say no to the wrong things. Eventually, the temptation will find you again, and you will respond with, "You've got to be kidding! I'm not going back. See what I have when I do life God's way?"

We get Him—closeness to Him—and a mission to help others. He calls us into a partnership with Himself in which we cooperate with His work in us, and then we use the principles He has taught us and we share them with others. Freedom shouldn't just stay with us. With God leading us, we can help others find freedom. See? Another reason not to go back.

If you're tempted to go back to a particular bondage, reread the article in this book that addresses it and search Scripture for strategies and motivations to say no. Keep saying yes to God's will for you, and depend on Him to implement His battle plan. He wants freedom for you even more than you do, and His love and power are strong enough to sustain freedom if you cooperate with His work in your life. Freedom is possible. Live the dream.

"Stand fast therefore in the liberty
by which Christ has made us free,
and do not be entangled again
with a yoke of bondage."
Galatians 5:1 NKJV

On Guard against Dangerous Distractions
by Rick Kauffman

Stay alert, stay focused, arrive alive.

Recently I discovered some alarming facts. I was researching roadway crash data for a presentation that I planned to make at a conference. In the US Department of Transportation's Fatal Accident Reporting System, the number one cause of death in the United States for people between the ages of 11 and 27 is motor vehicle crashes. The cost in terms of loss and suffering is incredible. The primary cause of these fatal crashes is believed to be distractions. We all know of numerous examples.

Forewarned is forearmed, or is it? As I thought about this, I considered the spiritual implications. Just as there are enemies of safe driving, believers encounter enemies of their spiritual walk. More than twenty of them have been discussed in this book.

Drivers are tasked to keep the vehicle on the road and avoid obstructions. Believers are tasked to follow Christ and grow in Him, to love God and others, and to serve the body of Christ. In other words, stay on God's path and avoid obstructions, including those that steer us into spiritual bondage. Our daily prayer could include: "Teach me Your way, O LORD, and lead me in a smooth path" (Psalm 27:11 NKJV*).

But the enemy is clever. He knows how to skillfully use a distraction. Through observation, the enemy learns how to manipulate us—how to get us to take our eyes off the "road" just long enough at the opportune moment to cause us to crash. Even though believers' souls are eternally free in Christ, safe from sin's price of spiritual death, Satan seeks to enslave us with fear, anger, or anxiety, with any tool he can use to destroy our spiritual health and peace. Whether his attack comes as a jolt from a major event or as a lull into complacency, it will come. But we can heed God's warning to counter his attack: "Be sober, be vigilant; because your adversary the devil walks about like a roaring lion, seeking whom he may devour" (1 Peter 5:8).

Drivers must develop skills to survive heavy traffic. They must stay focused and alert. So must we if we are to arrive at our spiritual "destinations" unchained and victorious. Dr. Adrian Rogers used to say, "The main thing is to keep the main thing, the main thing." Yes, but how? Dr. Charles Stanley has some of the best advice that I have ever heard: The first thing every morning, spend time in the word of God; take it in and think on it, it will prepare you for the trials of the day.

This wisdom is confirmed by God's principle for success: "This Book of the Law shall not depart from your mouth, but you shall meditate in it day and night, that you may observe to do according to all that is written in it. For then you will make your way prosperous, and then you will have good success" (Joshua 1:8).

I must admit that I haven't always done it, but when I do, it always works. God will prepare us for the day and for the distractions that we will face if we spend time with Him in Scripture. Although I may feel pressured by my schedule, in reality I am never too busy to spend time with God in His word. Jesus said, "If anyone loves Me, he will keep My word; and My Father will love him, and We will come to him and make Our home with him" (John 14:23). Spending time with God expresses our love for Him, but it also helps us to live according to His word in our daily walk, and it helps us to say no to seductive spiritual enemies that wield enslaving power.

May we not be distracted by the busyness of the world, by a preoccupation with the struggles of life, or by the tactics of the enemy. Our freedom in Christ is worth guarding. Let us be careful to stay close to God and to navigate life by the Road Map that He has given us—on guard against dangerous distractions.

*All Scripture verses are NKJV.

In Closing:
Finding Your Sanctuary
by Katy Kauffman

In the times when I've needed "sanctuary"—a place in Scripture of soothing words and strength-giving passages—I have turned to the book of Psalms. In my seventeen-year-old Bible, this comforting book is a rainbow menagerie of boxes, stars, arrows, circles, and dates, all drawing attention to life-altering, chain-breaking, darkness-dispelling verses. Some verses have five different dates next to them, indicating that these words of Scripture spoke to my heart again and again. Do you need a place of sanctuary when your heart grows weary from fighting life's spiritual battles? Let me share my favorite psalms with you, and I encourage you to find the place in Scripture that renews your heart.

My favorite chapter teeters between Psalm 91 and Psalm 107. Psalm 91 is the passage that God gave to my mother to reassure her that my great-grandmother, Barbara, was in heaven. My great-grandmother truly set her love upon God as verse 14 talks about. The chapter stirs our souls to trust God—the Almighty, the Most High—who delivers us from evil and covers us with His feathers. An excellent chapter for anyone who is battling seen or unseen forces.

My other favorite chapter is Psalm 107, a beautiful record of how God helped His people in "impossible" situations. In my Bible, blue and pink boxes surround the verses that are repeated, revealing a pattern. In this chapter, four scenarios show us how God rescues His people. In each scenario, the people cried out to God for help, He delivered them, and we learn what He did to rescue them exactly as they needed it. Each paragraph calls us to thank God for His goodness and His wonderful works done on our behalf.

Hidden in one of the paragraphs is a verse that wraps up our study on overcoming spiritual bondage. When we have been caught in a bondage for a while, it can feel like darkness hovers over us everywhere we go. Gloom becomes our sidekick, and hopelessness sets in. Our souls cry out for relief. But God ... He knows how to deliver us. Read the declaration of verse 14.

> "He brought them out of darkness and the shadow of death,
> and broke their chains in pieces."
> Psalm 107:14 NKJV*

Relief, hope, freedom. That's what God worked. Those who had rebelled against God found themselves in a bondage that only God could break. He allowed them to experience the result of their stubbornness—captivity—to get their attention. When the people cried out to Him for help, He answered. He answers us, too.

> "Oh, that men would give thanks to the LORD
> for His goodness, and for His wonderful works
> to the children of men!"
> Psalm 107:15

Are you free from the chains that have bound you? Praise God. Are you freer than you used to be? Thank Him for His work on your behalf. Are you still struggling with a particular bondage? Keep looking to God, and do what He tells you.

God works miracles. According to Psalm 107, God "satisfies the longing soul" (v.9), He "cuts the bars of iron in two" (v.16), He sends His Word and heals us and delivers us from our destructions (v.20), and He "calms the storm, so that its waves are still" (v.29). Run to Him. Ask Him to heal you and free you. Cooperate with

His work in your life. God makes freedom a reality.

"Whoever is wise will observe these things,
and they will understand the lovingkindness of the LORD."
Psalm 107:43

*All Scripture verses are NKJV.

The Healing
by Katy Kauffman

The ache I've felt in my soul
The desire to be made whole
The longings that have gone unmet
The pain I want to forget

A Healer I've needed and prayed for
The Calmer of the stormy roar
My Hero in difficult battles
The Releaser of chains and shackles

Hope starts to sing once again
He rides on the wings of the wind
The Healer reaches in and holds my heart
Breathes life and healing into every part

The pain and anguish have been soothed
The darkness cries and begins to move
Out of my heart and out of my life
My soul rejoices to find the light

I can stand up again, straight and tall
He holds my hand, lest I fall
I lean on Him, my Healer and Guide
My heavenly Father who will provide

He will keep His promises, they will come true
I will give Him my all, He'll see me through
The troubling and uncertain times that lie ahead
My heart is now safe, my soul is fed

His fellowship will see me through dark valleys
His presence will brighten lonesome alleys
My heart beats strongly once again
In Him I have a faithful friend

I'm ready to love others and share the truth
My story of pain and healing is the proof
That He's real and catches every tear
That He heals those who to Him draw near

My heart is ready to do great feats
For His name as He makes me complete
This joy I've never known before
This love I will cherish forevermore

Contributing Authors

Contributing Authors
In Alphabetical Order

Erin Elizabeth Austin is the founder of Broken but Priceless Ministries, a non-profit organization which helps caregivers and people suffering with a chronic illness. In her spare time, she loves to spend time with family, friends, and build forts with her nephews. Her goal for each day is to have an adventure, laugh, love, and eat chocolate. Connect with her at www.brokenbutpriceless.com.

Cherrilynn Bisbano is a speaker, teacher, and writer. She is a Volunteer Associate Editor at *Almost an Author*, and has written for several online magazines. Her ministry is to encourage her brothers and sisters in Christ to be all that God created them to be. She has been married for 18 years and has one son. You can connect with her at her blog: truthtoshine.blogspot.com.

Lauren Craft enjoys writing about how living for Christ is abundant life (John 10:10), filled with purpose, joy, and lasting hope. She loves serving as a missions leader in her church in Virginia. In addition to writing, Lauren works as a magazine and book editor and proofreads Bible translation materials for Wycliffe Associates. Connect with her at www.laurencraftauthor.com.

Trina Dofflemyer has served as an adjunct professor of Biblical studies, leadership mentor, retreat leader, and writer. She currently serves in an apologetic ministry and loves all things theology, hiking with family, reading, and drinking tea. Connect with her on her blog at EnduringLeaders.com, or on Twitter (@TrinaDofflemyer) and Facebook (@EnduringLeaders).

Rosemarie Fitzsimmons is a retired U.S. Marine gunnery sergeant, a wife, and the mother of two boys. She blogs as the *Portrait Writer* and enjoys meeting ordinary people with extraordinary stories. Her award-winning book, *Caged Sparrow*, is a true, modern-day Joseph story of a tough Buffalo, New York cop falsely imprisoned and forever changed by Jesus' healing touch. Follow her blog at https://rosethestoryteller.com, or via Twitter (@pjoy93).

In addition to being an active writer, speaker, teacher, and blogger, Ron Gallagher serves in a variety of roles as a ministry consultant for local churches. His Biblical insights are coupled with down-to-earth humor, satire, and relevant stories, all aimed at promoting "right side up thinking in an upside down world." Check out Ron's blog, *Gallagher's Pen* at https://gallagherspen.com.

Tessa Emily Hall writes inspirational yet authentic YA fiction. Her passion for shedding light on clean entertainment and media for teens led her to a career as a Jr. Agent at Hartline Literary, Editor for Illuminate YA (LPC imprint), and Founder/Editor for PursueMagazine.net. Her favorite way to procrastinate is by connecting with readers. Find out more on her website: www.tessaemilyhall.com.

Award-winning blogger and speaker, Ginger Harrington shares heart, hope, and a dash of humor. A Marine veteran wife and mom to three young adults, Ginger's keeping faith fresh at GingerHarrington.com. Helping to create a ministry for women in the military community, Ginger speaks, writes, and oversees publishing at PlantingRoots.net.

Beebe Kauffman is a co-founder of Lighthouse Bible Studies and the chief editor of its online magazine, *Refresh*. She has written *Isaiah: Setting Things Right* and is currently writing a book of application for the New Testament called *A Whole Lot of Wonderful—the New Testament*. She loves photographing flowers, making Christmas cards, drinking good coffee, and watching Facebook videos of animals.

Katy Kauffman is a Bible teacher, an award-winning author, and a co-founder of Lighthouse Bible Studies. She is an editor and a designer of *Refresh Bible Study Magazine*. Her Bible studies for women focus on winning life's spiritual battles. She loves spending time with family and friends, making jewelry, and connecting with writers and readers. Connect with her at http://lighthousebiblestudies.com.

Because Rick Kauffman is a lighting engineer, his boss told him to "Go light the world." That's his mission in ministry, too. Rick is a co-founder of Lighthouse Bible Studies, which he started with his wife Beebe and daughter Katy. Visit http://lighthousebiblestudies.com/rickkauffman   to see his speaking topics and teaching series. His first book of Biblical application, *1 Kings 1-11: Stay under God's Leadership*, releases in 2017.

Leigh Powers is the author of *Renewed: A 40-Day Devotional for Healing from Church Hurt and Loving Well in Ministry* (FaithWords, November 2017). She is passionate about seeing lives changed as we encounter God through His word. A pastor's wife, freelance writer, and mother of three, she strives to combine solid Biblical study with real-world application. She blogs at *My Life. His Story.* (www.Leighpowers.com).

Denise Roberts loves a good cup of coffee with friends, snuggles from her chocolate lab, doing life with her husband, being a mom to grown-up kids, and most of all, encouraging others to connect with the life-giving and life-sustaining Word of God in the messy places of our lives. Connect with Denise at www.deniseroberts.org and on Facebook at Denise Roberts – Living Holy.

Josie Siler shares God's gifts of beauty, hope, and adventure at josiesiler.com. When she's not writing or taking pictures, you'll find this biker chick riding her motorcycle, reading a good book, drinking coffee, eating chocolate, or shooting something at the range. Josie is also Vice President of Broken but Priceless Ministries and Editorial Assistant of *Broken but Priceless: The Magazine*.

Lorphine St Louis was born and raised in La Gonave, Haiti. When she was 19, God opened the doors for her to immigrate to the United States where she met and fell in love with her husband, Pierre, and they now have 3 beautiful children. Lorphine co-founded Future Generation International Missions Inc., and she is the Director of Faith House Orphanage where she is raising 30 girls. Connect with her at http://www.fgimwitness.org.

Jeannie Waters loves sharing encouragement face-to-face and through writing devotions and articles. She is a wife, mom, grandmother, and retired teacher who currently teaches English as a Second Language at a local college. She adores picnics, mountain streams, and meeting new people.

Laura W. Watts is a pastor's wife, speaker, Bible teacher, and writer who works full-time as the CFO for the SC Department of Revenue. She is co-founder of Full Course Ministries and desires to see fellow believers experience abundant life in Jesus. Follow Laura on Twitter (@setfreewatts), on Facebook (Laura W. Watts), and at www.fullcourseministries.com.

Evelyn Wells has a passion to glorify God by writing inspirational material, including devotions, creative nonfiction, and short stories. She is currently serving as a District Director of Lay Servant Ministries in the United Methodist Church. She enjoys a good book, her two cats, and traveling to the coast. She lives in North Georgia near her children and grandson.

Adria Wilkins writes and speaks about how what's in our "box" called life is often unexpected. After suffering the unthinkable—death of three-year-old Blake—Adria found that Jesus sustains and even surprises His followers with joy. She is writing a collection of short pieces called *Joy Box Stories* pointing to that conclusion. She lives in Virginia with her family. Connect with her at https://www.facebook.com/joyboxstories.

Wife, mom, and latte junkie, Tina Yeager has won sixteen writing awards, including FCWC's 2013 Writer of the Year. Inspirational speaker and online life coach, she loves to offer encouragement through words. Her YA supernatural series launches with *Inscaping*. For coaching or more written content, visit her for a virtual cup of java at divineencouragement.com and tyeagerwrites.com.

Other Books Available from Lighthouse Bible Studies

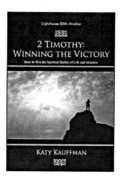

2 Timothy: Winning the Victory
How to Win the Spiritual Battles
of Life and Ministry
by Katy Kauffman

Isaiah: Setting Things Right
Chapters 1-6 How can we cooperate with God
to set things right in our hearts, minds,
and daily lives?
by Beebe Kauffman

From Lighthouse Bible Studies

Faith, Courage, and Victory
The Stories, Struggles, and Triumphs
of 24 Characters of the Bible
by Katy Kauffman

A Whole Lot of Wonderful—
the Gospel of Matthew
What Does the Bible Say,
What Does It Mean, and How Is It
Relevant to Life Today?
by Beebe Kauffman

Connect with Us
We would love to hear from you!

The mission of Lighthouse Bible Studies
is to connect people to God
through His Word.

E-mail us at
lighthousebiblestudies@hotmail.com
to subscribe to our free online magazine,
Refresh Bible Study Magazine.

Visit us at
lighthousebiblestudies.com.

Find us on:
Facebook: Lighthouse Bible Studies
Facebook: Refresh Bible Study Magazine
Twitter: @KatyKauffman28

CPSIA information can be obtained
at www.ICGtesting.com
Printed in the USA
FFOW01n1631080417
34297FF